Children's Bulletin
Idea Book

Children's Bulletin Idea Book

Faye Fredricks, Nellie deVries,
and Annetta Dellinger

Cheryl Strikwerda Randall, Illustrator

BAKER BOOK HOUSE
Grand Rapids, Michigan 49516

ISBN: 0-8010-3536-8

Second printing, December 1988

Printed in the United States of America

CONTENTS

Guidelines

Now that your church has decided to offer children's bulletins, you're probably wondering, "Where do we begin?" The obvious answer is, "At the beginning."

The first thing to be considered is the goal of your bulletin program. It is fairly easy to keep children occupied during the services with a few pictures to color or quizzes to complete. But if you want your bulletins to help the children understand the service, make them feel that they are a part of it, and also make them aware of the church family, your bulletins will take on a different perspective.

Involve the pastor as you plan the theme each week. Know what the sermon title is and, if possible, some of the topics that will be covered in the sermon. Check with the choir leader(s) to see if they have any special announcements for children. The adult bulletin of the previous week will announce special meetings and offerings for the next Sunday. These items can help the children to be aware of church activities.

A very special part of the bulletin will involve the children themselves. A welcome to a baby brother or sister, or a new family joining the church, a listing of the children who had birthdays that week, mentioning which children are in the hospital or have had surgery (tonsillectomy), and featuring a mystery child are ways to make the children feel that they have a bulletin designed especially for them. The mentioning of children's names creates an interest that cannot be duplicated elsewhere. Ask the children to prepare special cards for those who are sick. Ask them to pray for special needs and to thank God for answers to prayers.

You may want to ask the children to design a cover for special days or to prepare a puzzle or quiz. Jokes and riddles can occasionally be included, also.

But the most important thing is the sermon topic. Be creative in the ways to involve children in listening. Perhaps a fill-in quiz or a list of words to listen for will help. You may want to refer to hymns or anthems the congregation or choirs will be singing. Try to keep the theme of the day in mind. Sometimes that is well-nigh impossible and then a "generic" or "ready-to-use" bulletin may be the answer.

Now that your goals are established, you're ready to move on to personnel. Who will prepare the bulletin? You may want to ask the Christian Education Director or Youth Pastor to have the sole responsibility. This can also be worked out well by a committee, provided one or two members have the assignment for a specified block of time. Rotate the months so that the same people are not always responsible for the same special days, such as Easter, Christmas, or Thanksgiving. You may be fortunate enough to have one person with talent and preferably also a computer who is willing to tackle the assignment. Perhaps you have volunteered or have been appointed. Enthusiasm, creativity, and a sensitivity to children and the purpose of worship are the key ingredients for the editor(s) of a church bulletin.

The equipment available in your church will determine how you prepare the bulletin. If a stencil must be cut, that may limit the kind of art you can use. Perhaps the bulletin can be photocopied (courtesy of a member businessman) or printed (courtesy of a local printer). That will make your job easier.

Use the grids we've prepared to lay out the bulletin. A local printer can prepare copies of the grid in nonreproducing blue ink. Type and drawings can easily be placed on the blue lines and the lines will not show on the completed bulletin. The grids make it so much easier to get a neat bulletin. Use rubber cement to paste. It is easy to use and clean up.

How should the bulletin be laid out? There should be a careful balance between a set format for easy recognition and good variety for interest. A logo or design featuring the name of your church (Millbrook Morning Glories, Georgetown Sunbeams) is a good idea.

Typewriter type tends to be a little stilted for children but can be used to give directions. Handlettering works well. Children love to color in outline letters or fill in missing spaces in the letters. The grids will help avoid lettering that is poorly spaced or crooked.

For more ideas, exchange bulletins with neighboring churches or write to Faye Fredricks (7118 Williamstown Dr., Hudsonville, Michigan 49426) to enroll in her exchange program. Logos Art (see address below) provides excellent materials for bulletins. Comb the activity book section of your local bookstore for ideas. Be sure to follow copyright restrictions listed. Some publishers will allow local church use without charge. Avoid using greeting cards, comics, or children's page items from a local newspaper. That material is covered by stringent copyright laws. So is coloring book art.

Assemble your materials into a workable filing system. The first section should be a "Current Week Information" file. It could contain items such as last week's adult bulletin (for upcoming events), offering schedule, pastor's preaching schedule, information on contact persons (choir director, church school leader). You may wish to include a file for each of the following items:

Current Week Information
Quizzes (various types)
Birthday, Music, Library, Birth Announcements
Lord's Supper
Baptism
Profession of Faith
Fillers (miscellaneous general quizzes used to complete
    bulletins—fill in spaces)
Heidelberg Catechism (or Westminster Catechism)
Worship—quizzes about parts of service
Passion Week
Christmas
Prayer
Missions
Basic Truths, Gifts, Fruits of the Spirit
Old Testament
New Testament
Reformation Day/Hunger Awareness
Bible, Ten Commandments
Pentecost/Ascension Day

Seasons
Parables
Offerings/Agency Handouts
Holidays
Expressive Faces
Trim
Nature
Grid Paper
General Pictures
Cross Reference File of Ideas and Bible Verses

The children of the congregation love to be involved in bulletin preparation and distribution. Choose one or two children to be assistant editors and rotate the assignment. The assistant editors can help to plan the contents, select the borders, arrange the art, and if capable, under your supervision, do the layout. Be sure to list the names of the assistant editors in the bulletins they prepare. Select children (alphabetically is a good system) to distribute the bulletins to children of the congregation as they arrive on Sunday morning. Their names can also be listed in the bulletin. The idea is to get as many names as possible into the bulletin. Everyone, child or adult, likes to see his or her name in print.

Allow for additional activities in bulletins occasionally. Include extra paper so that cards or letters can be prepared. Arrange for handy collection of the items and be sure to thank the children for making them. That is an excellent way to remember sick, shut-ins, senior citizens, as well as the pastor, and even the President or Prime Minister.

The church family corner can be a meaningful introduction to the practice of caring about fellow members. List prayer concerns and invite children to make a card or draw a picture for the people involved. The "mystery person" feature is an excellent way to introduce the shy child or the quiet one who is usually overlooked. Offer a prize (a bookmark) to the first person to correctly identify the mystery person and also give a bookmark to the mystery person. Often the mystery corner is the first item checked by the children. Be sure to credit both the puzzle solver and the mystery person in the next week's bulletin.

Occasionally you may wish to insert a bookmark or other advertising material distributed by the agency for which the offering is being given. A picture of a missionary family, especially if it includes their children, is a good way to create interest in missions.

101 Bible Activity Sheets and *Bible Activity Sheets for Special Days*, both published by Baker Book House and available from the publisher or at your local Christian bookstore, contain excellent material for children's bulletin use. *The Sunday School Clip Art Book* published by Gospel Light Publications (Ventura, CA 93006) has a great assortment of art. The firms listed below also offer helpful materials in bulletin preparation:

Shining Star Publications
Box 299
Carthage, IL 62321-0299

Crown National Bureau
424 N. Third St.
Burlington, IA 52601

Artmaster
550 North Claremont Blvd.
Claremont, CA 91711

Logos Art Productions, Inc.
346 Chester St.
St. Paul, MN 55107

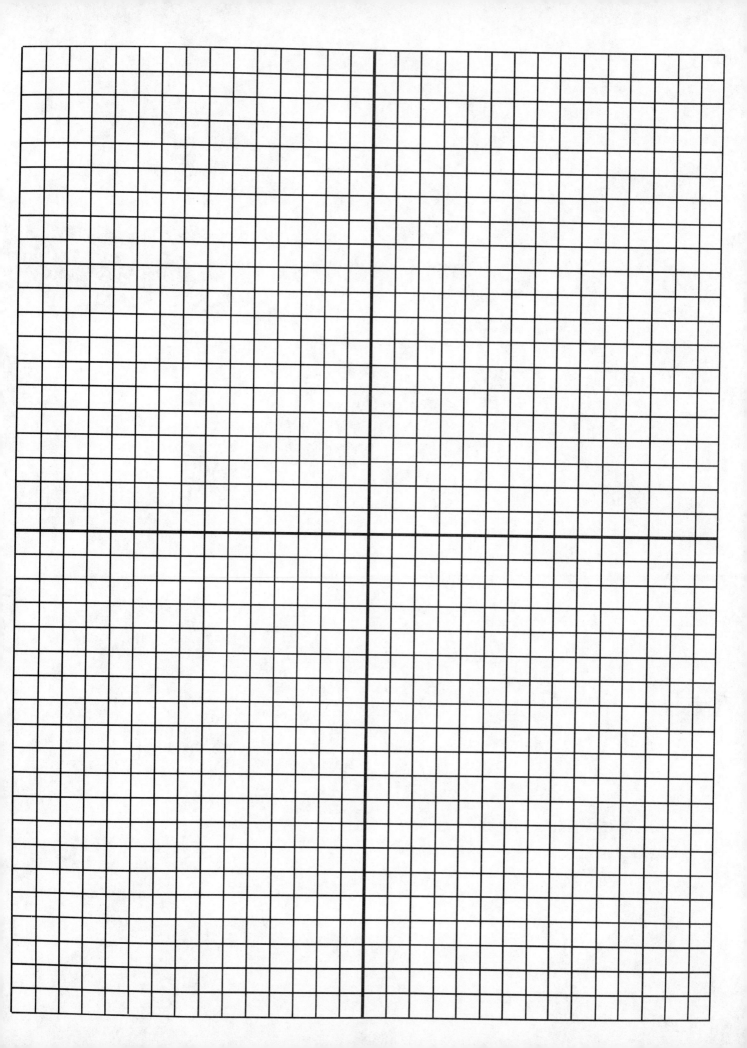

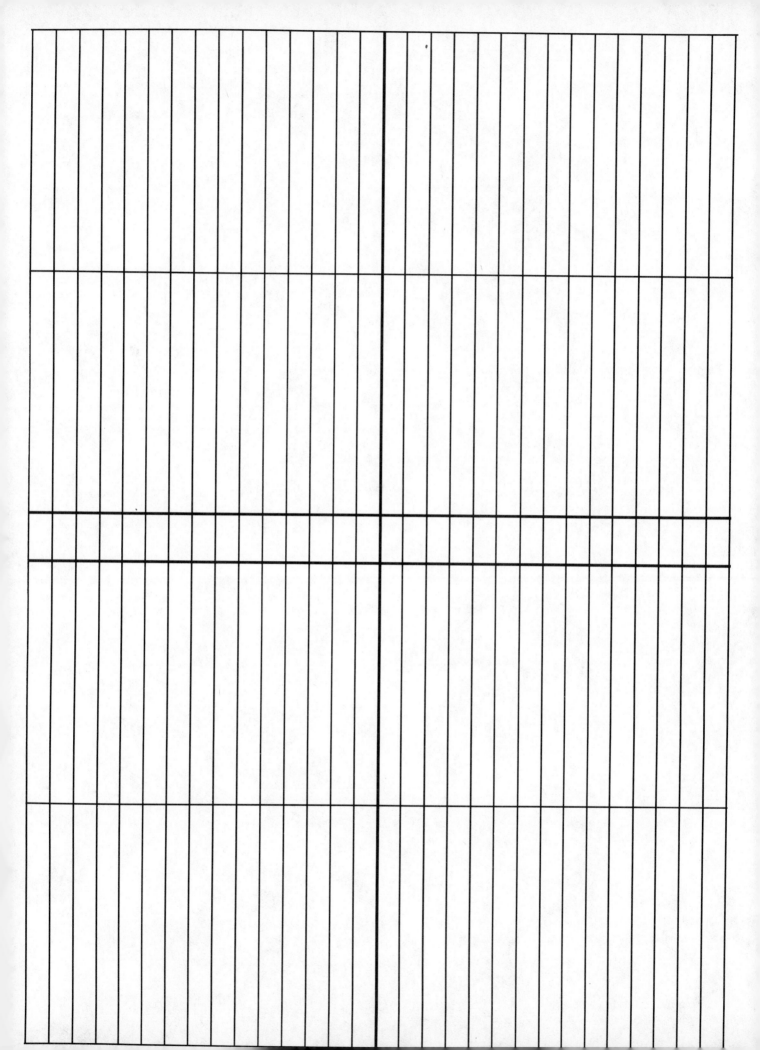

Ready-to-Use Bulletins

CHILDREN'S BULLETIN

The Child Jesus

Luke 2:21-40

When Jesus was 8 days old Mary and Joseph presented Him at the temple. Two old people, Anna and Simeon, were very happy to see their Messiah. Simeon sang a song of praise about it.

Find 12 musical notes hidden in our picture.

When Jesus was 12 years old, He went to Jerusalem with His parents for a festival. The maze shows the path from His parents to the Temple.

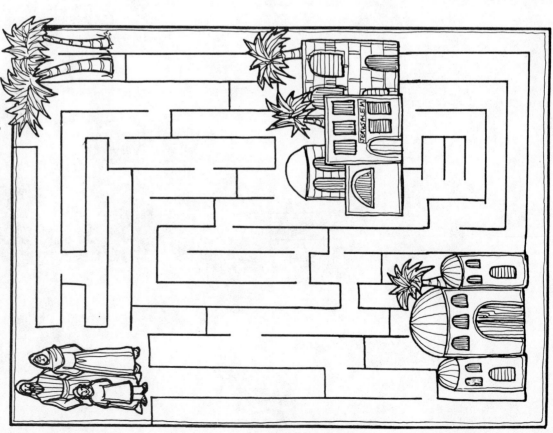

After Herod died, an angel told Joseph . . .

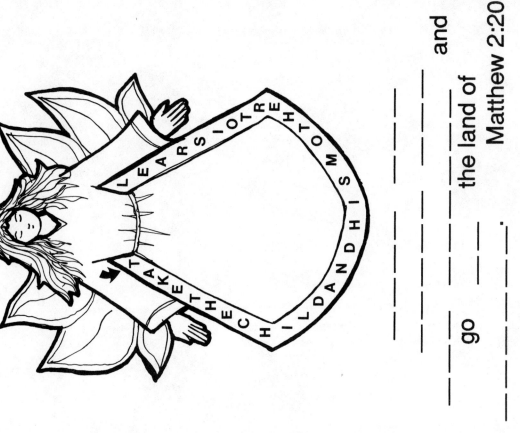

go _____ _____ and

_____ the land of

_____ . Matthew 2:20

**Start at arrow. Write down every letter to
find the angel's message.**

King Herod wanted to kill Jesus so
Mary, Joseph, and Jesus fled to Egypt.

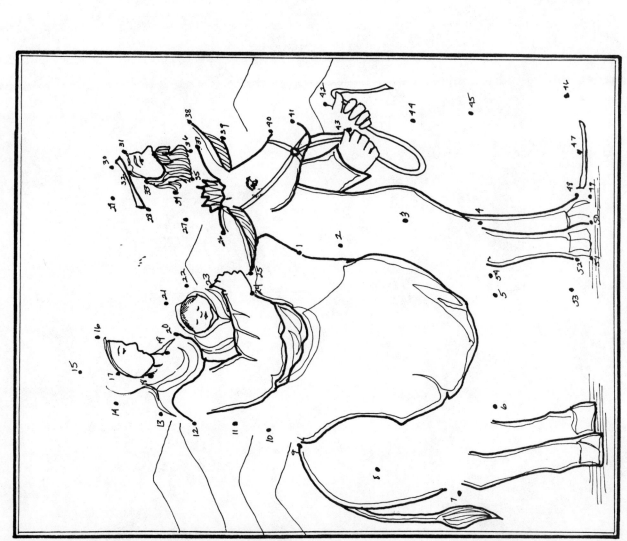

CHILDREN'S BULLETIN

Jesus Loves the Little Children

Jesus said, "Let the little children come to me."

Jesus raised Jairus's daughter from the dead.

Feeding of the 5,000

In John 6 we read that Jesus fed 5,000 people from one small boy's lunch of 5 loaves and 2 fish. After everyone had eaten there were 12 baskets filled with left-overs.

Find the 12 baskets hidden in our picture. Color the picture.

CHILDREN'S BULLETIN

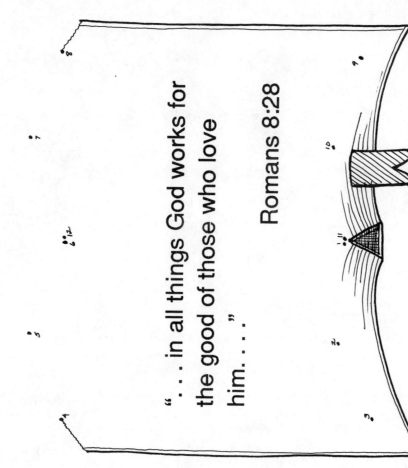

" . . . in all things God works for the good of those who love him. . . . "

Romans 8:28

Find Romans. It is in the _____ Testament. Romans 8:28 is on page _____ of your Bible.

JESUS LOVES YOU

Draw a picture of yourself.

FOLLOW THE DOTS

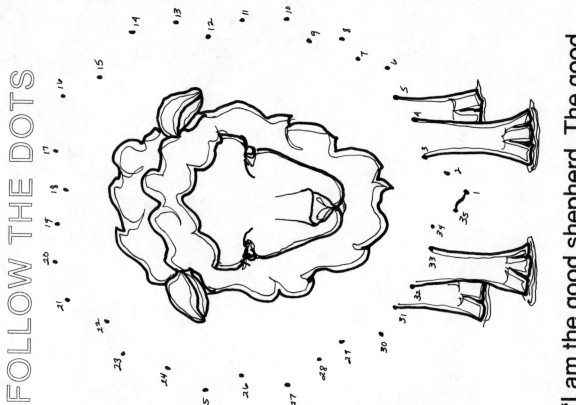

"I am the good shepherd. The good shepherd lays down his life for the sheep."

John 10:11

Finish this sentence: "Let the _____ come to me and do not hinder (stop) them." Luke 18:16

CHILDREN'S BULLETIN

SUMMERTIME

R
O
D
E
H
T
S
L

OF
ALL

The letters on the balloons help spell words. Follow the string down to the blank and put that letter on the blank.

Follow the right path to put ice cream in your cone. Underline your favorite flavor.

FLAVOR OF THE MONTH

chocolate	raspberry royale
vanilla	double choc. fudge
chocolate chip	rocky road
butter pecan	pralines + cream
heavenly hash	rainbow sherbet

CHILDREN'S BULLETIN

MERRY CHRISTMAS!

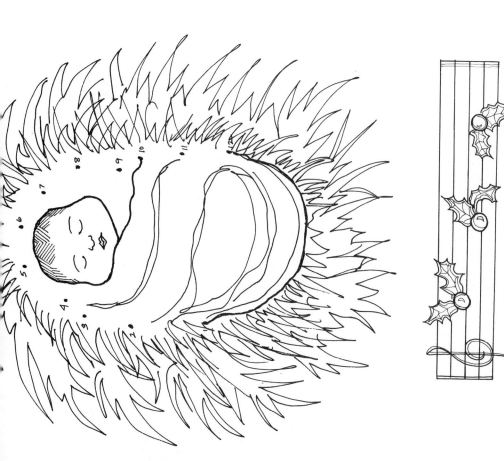

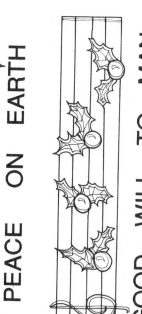

PEACE ON EARTH

GOOD WILL TO MAN

Christmas

The very first Christmas gift was from God. That Gift was His Son, Jesus.

Draw a picture of baby Jesus. Next, draw you beside the baby.

THE BIRTH OF JESUS
Matthew 2:1-18; Luke 2:40-52

Draw a line from the names below to the correct statement.

CAESAR AUGUSTUS   City where Jesus was born.

JOSEPH   Mother of Jesus.

NAZARETH   City where Joseph and Mary lived.

BETHLEHEM   He said the world should be taxed.

MARY   They followed a star.

SHEPHERDS   He held Jesus in the temple and praised God.

ANGEL   Visited Jesus in the stable.

SIMEON   Joseph, Mary and Jesus fled to this place.

ANNA   Means savior.

JESUS   Brought the message of Jesus' birth.

WISE MEN   The king who wanted to kill Jesus.

EGYPT   Husband of Mary.

HEROD   City where Jesus was brought to the temple.

JERUSALEM   An old prophetess who saw the baby Jesus.

CHILDREN'S BULLETIN

HAPPY EASTER!

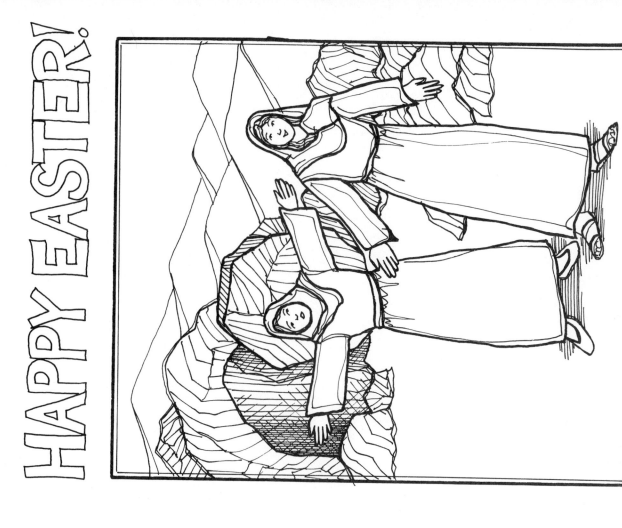

Chr__st
th__ L__rd__s
r__s__n
__d !
__

= a   = e   = i   = o   = y

EASTER

Complete the verse below by using the letters from the word "Easter."

"Y_ SEEK JE_US WHO W_S CRUCIFIED HE IS NO_ HERE: FOR HE IS _ISEN, AS H_ SAID." MATTHEW 28

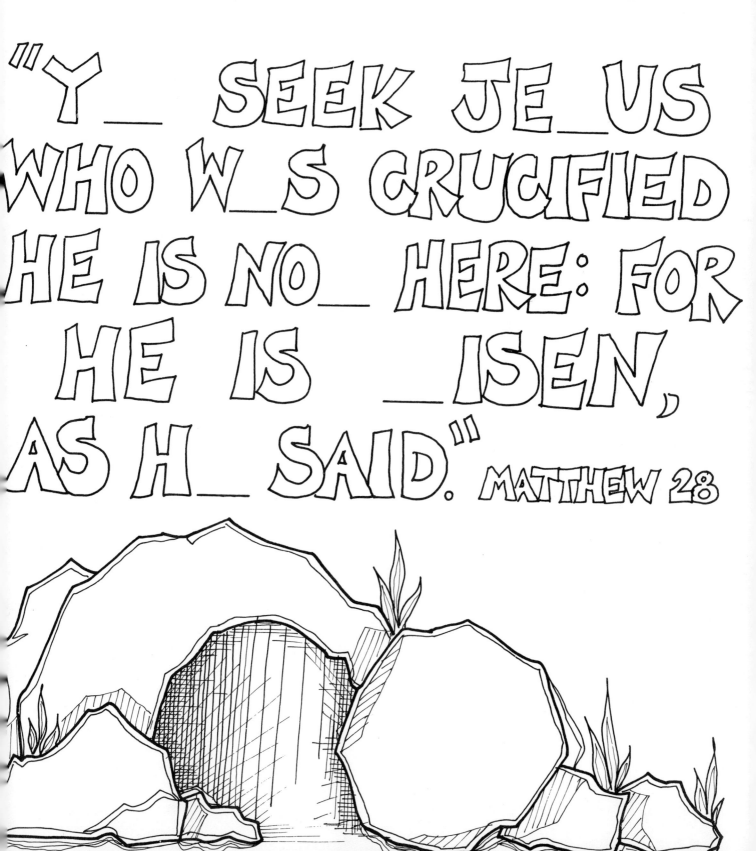

CHILDREN'S BULLETIN
THANKSGIVING

Connect the dots to find a picture of
someone who thanked God long ago.

The fourth Thursday in November is proclaimed by the President of the United States to be a Day of Thanksgiving to God by the people of our nation. God really has blessed our country. As Christians we always thank God for His goodness. List one of God's gifts to you on each of the tail feathers of the turkey on this bulletin cover.

Two ways to draw turkeys:

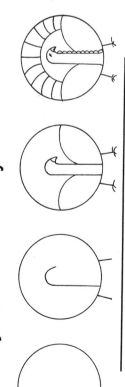

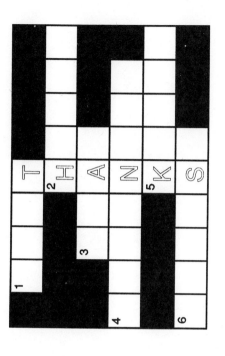

Trace around your hand. Add the legs and feet to the bottom.

Turn the thumb into a head by an eye, a bill and a wavy line to the neck.

Try these at home!

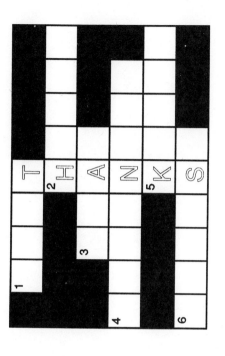

Fill in the blanks with the correct words.

1. "Thanks be to God for his indescribable _____." (2 Corinthians 9:15)

2. Thanks and _____ be to our God. (Revelation 7:12)

3. "We always thank God . . . when we _____ for you." (Colossians 1:3)

4. "I thank Jesus Christ . . . who has given me _____ . . ." (1 Timothy 1:12)

5. "For this reason I _____ before the Father." (Ephesians 3:14)

6. "Give thanks to him and _____ his name." (Psalm 100:4b)

CHILDREN'S BULLETIN

THE PRODIGAL SON

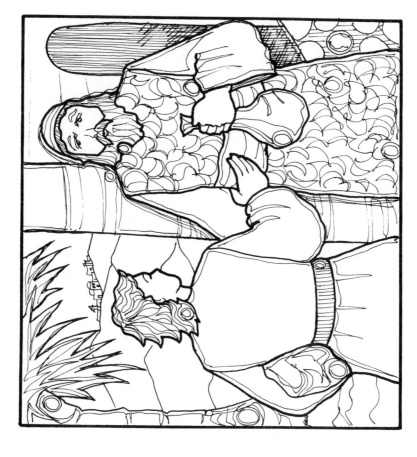

In Luke 15:11-31 Jesus told the story of the prodigal son. In the story the younger son asked for his inheritance.

Find 15 coins hidden in the picture.

When his father saw him coming, he ran to his son and kissed him.
He gave him a robe, a ring, sandals, and had a feast for him.

Draw the son's gift on him. Draw a feast table in the background.

God welcomes us when we come to him, too.

When he left home and had money, he had lots of friends and fun. Soon his money and friends were gone. He was lonely, poor and hungry. He got a job feeding pigs.

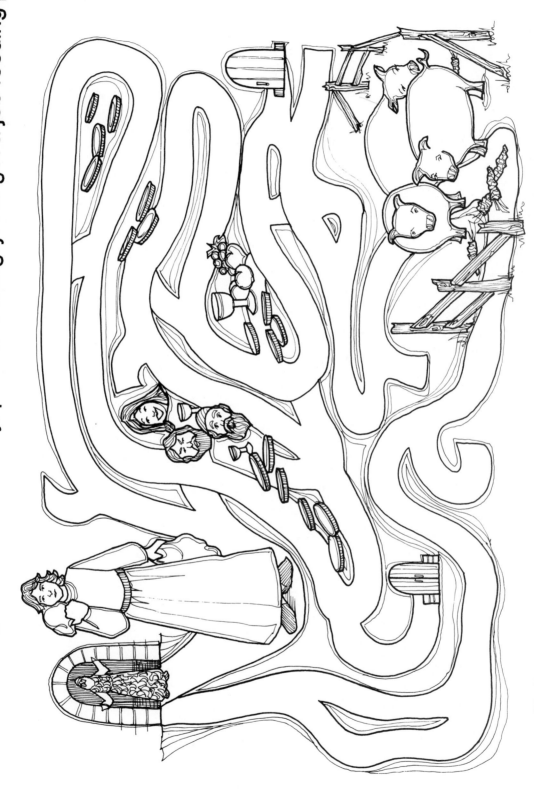

Follow the young man as he leaves home. Work him through the maze and get him home again.

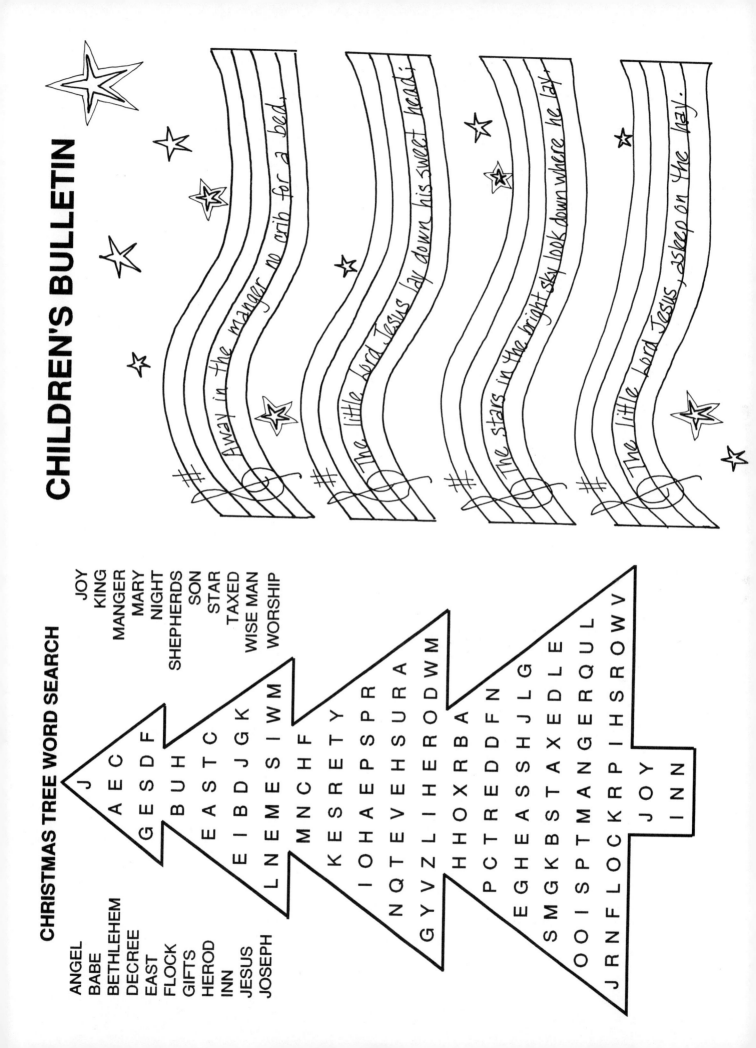

CHILDREN'S BULLETIN

Away in the manger no crib for a bed,

The little Lord Jesus lay down his sweet head;

The stars in the bright sky look down where he lay,

The little Lord Jesus, asleep on the hay.

CHRISTMAS TREE WORD SEARCH

ANGEL
BABE
BETHLEHEM
DECREE
EAST
FLOCK
GIFTS
HEROD
INN
JESUS
JOSEPH
JOY
KING
MANGER
MARY
NIGHT
SHEPHERDS
SON
STAR
TAXED
WISE MAN
WORSHIP

```
                    J
                  A E C
                G E S D F
                  B U H
              E A S T C
            E I B D J G K
          L N E M E S I W M
            M N C H F
          K E S R E T Y
        I O H A E P S P R
      N Q T E V E H S U R A
    G Y V Z L I H E R O D W M
        H H O X R B A
      P C T R E D D F N
    E G H E A S S H J L G
  S M G K B S T A X E D L E
O O I S P T M A N G E R Q U L
J R N F L O C K R P I H S R O W V
              J O Y
              I N N
```

Words that can be found in today's message Luke 2:1-7. Draw a line to the correct answer.

1. Decree   a. take in marriage
2. Linage   b. a place to stay
3. Swaddling   c. an order or law
4. Taxed   d. strips of long cloth
5. Espoused   3. descendant
6. Inn   f. payment of money

Unscramble the names below to find key people in Christ's birth.

1. Ryam _____
2. Sujes _____
3. Baliteezh _____
4. Hichazare _____

5. Nojh _____
6. Peohjs _____
7. Rehdshsep _____

Color the squares that are blank and find a special name. (Hint . . . we're celebrating His birthday TODAY!)

Starting with the letter "F," use every other letter, go around twice.

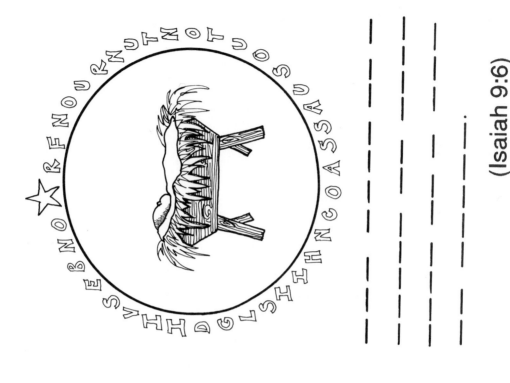

__ __ __ __ __ __ __ __ __ __

__ __ __ __ __ __ __ __ __ __ .

(Isaiah 9:6)

CHILDREN'S BULLETIN

Women in the Bible

Search for Bible wives:

```
Z A O P B S R E H T O M S A R A H R T L
P R I S C I L L A U C P S D W H A E E E
S W E J A B I G A I L E V E A T N H F A
E H G E V P E L I T N E G K I U N T J J
V A K Z I P P O R A H L E M P R A S N M
I L L E A H O H T T P B A T H S H E B A
W G P B B Z O H I Q E L I S A B E T H R
S E T E L E H C A R U D E B E H C O J Y
V M I L C A H W X N A O M I C H A L Y A
```

Abigail	Asenath
Eglah	Elisabeth
Eve	Hannah
Jezebel	Jochebed
Mary	Milcah
Naomi	Priscilla
Rebekah	Ruth
Sarah	Zipporah

Bathsheba
Esther
Jael
Leah
Michal
Rachel
Sapphira

PICTURE STUDY

Match each picture to a Bible verse. Each picture means something special in the story of Esther.

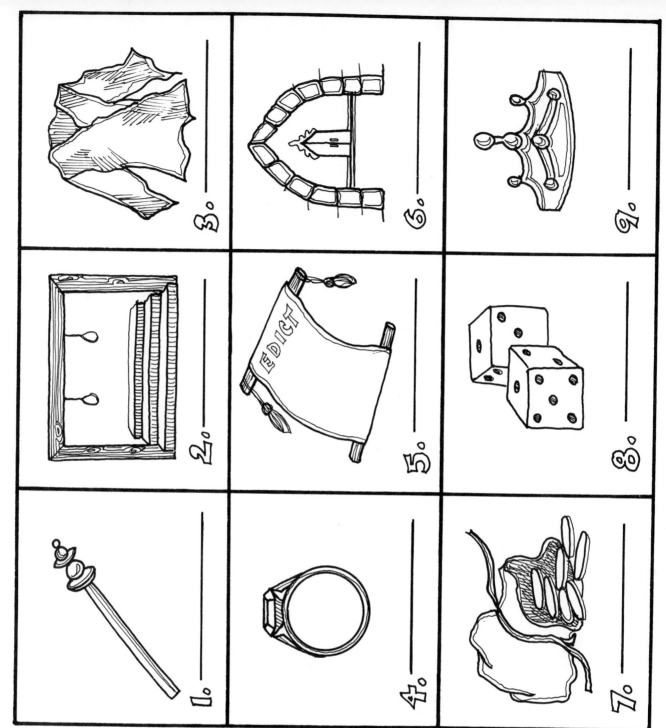

1. _____

2. _____

3. _____

4. _____

5. _____

6. _____

7. _____

8. _____

9. _____

Esther 4:1-3
Esther 5:2
Esther 8:1-2
Esther 5:9-13
Esther 7:10
Esther 2:17
Esther 3:12-14
Esther 3:7
Esther 3:8-9

CHILDREN'S BULLETIN

GOD KEEP YOU IN HIS CARE

FAMILIES

Our families are very important.

In our families, God show us His special care.

Let's thank Him for our families right now.

Dear God, Thank you for our families, and for your special care for us. For Jesus sake, Amen.

This morning's sermon is titled "WHY?" When bad things happened to Job, he questioned if God still cared for him. The answer was always Yes. God always cares for His people.

And He will always care for you too!

Find the hidden words from Job 1

```
R
B H B
D O G N P
Q R J F E A V
B S O X E N R E S
  V L H B C H O
  S A T A N
  H S E
  A
```

Job   God
Oxen   Lord
Satan   Sheep

God really does care for His people. And not just adults only. One day, when His disciples chased the children away because they thought that Jesus was too busy, He said to them, "Don't do that! Let the children come to me, for my kingdom belongs to them!"

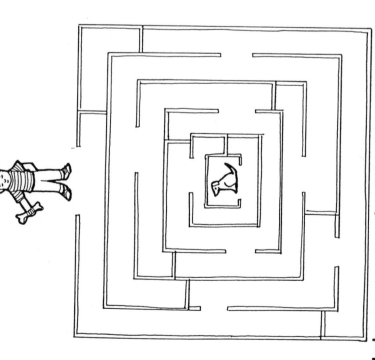

Johnny cares for his puppy too! He wants to find him. Can you help?

CHILDREN'S BULLETIN

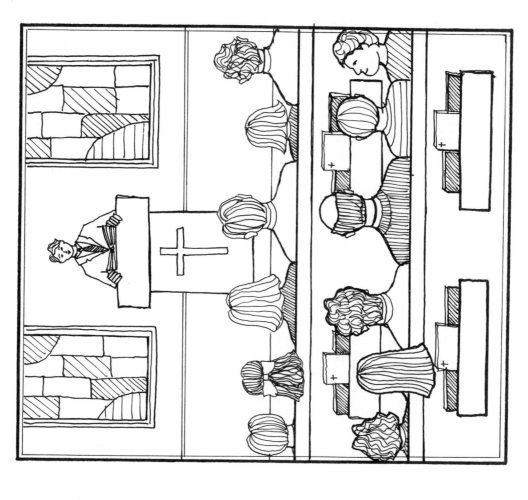

Do not forget My day. Be happy with My Word and do what I ask.

How can we do this?

Look at the word clues. Pick the word and write it on the line.

God wants us to _____ His
(here   hear)

Word, _____ out what He wants
(find   fined)

and then _____ works that please
(due   do)

Him. He wants us to _____ as His
(lid   live)

children with His Word in _____
(our   hour)

hearts, on our _____ , and in our
(lisps   lips)

_____ .
(ears   airs)

SUNDAY

A SPECIAL DAY!

We come to church to worship God because we love Him. Write a note to God telling Him why you love Him.

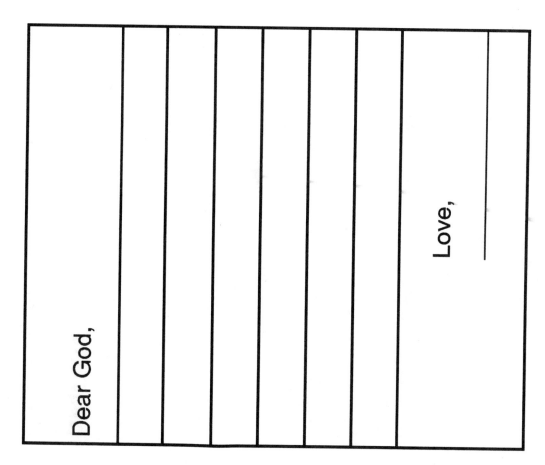

Dear God,

Love, _____

CHILDREN'S BULLETIN

PRAYER

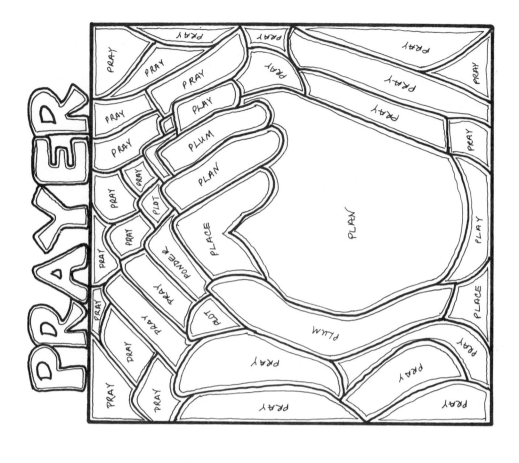

Color all the spaces with the word "pray" in them.

Put the letters in **Prayer** in order in the boxes below.

Monday ☐ ray for the hungry people today.

Tuesday ☐ emember to pray and read your Bible today.

Wednesday ☐ prayer for our church should be raised today.

Thursday ☐ our family needs your prayers today.

Friday ☐ ven if you're busy, take time to pray today.

Saturday ☐ emember to thank God today for all the blessings of the week.

Dial-a-Verse to see what God tells us in 1 Thessalonians 5:17.

Let your fingers do the walking . . . .

The first # under a line tells you what # to look at on the dial. The 1, 2, or 3 tells you what letter you need in that circle on the dial. Example: 6-2=N. Get it? HAPPY DIALING!

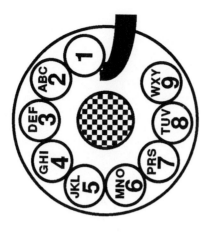

" ___ ___ ___ ___ ___ ___ ___ ___ ___ ___ ___ ___ ___ ___
2-3 6-3 6-2 8-1 4-3 6-2 8-2 2-1 5-3 5-3 9-3

7-1 7-2 2-1 9-3 "

Do you know any other verses about prayer?

_____

_____

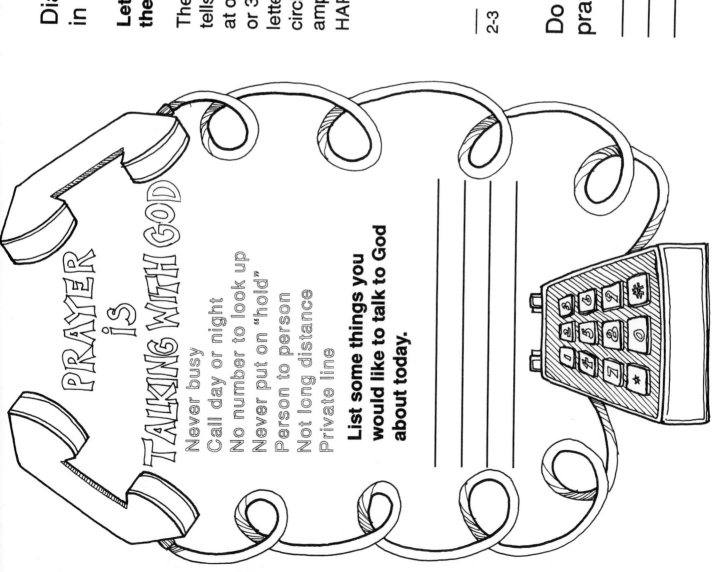

PRAYER
is
TALKING WITH GOD

Never busy
Call day or night
No number to look up
Never put on "hold"
Person to person
Not long distance
Private line

List some things you would like to talk to God about today.

_____

_____

_____

CHILDREN'S BULLETIN

LIFE IS PRECIOUS

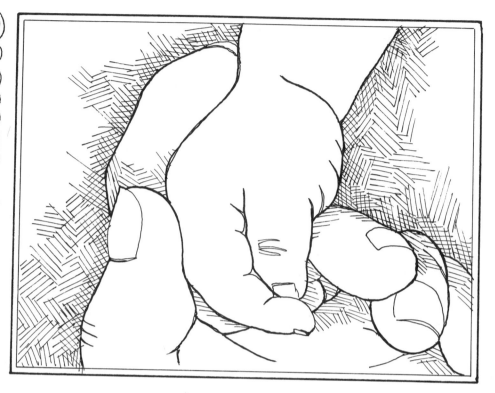

The Ten Commandments say, "You shall not kill." But Jesus said, "Love your neighbor, as much as you love yourself."

Surely we don't kill, but do we love enough?

Ask God to help you love more.

Our bulletin today reminds us how precious human life is, and how we should never do anything to harm it. We are also told to avoid hate and anger toward other people.

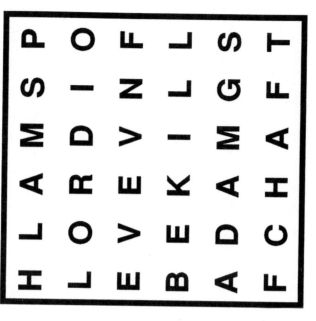

H	L	A	M	S	P
L	O	R	D	I	O
E	V	E	V	N	F
B	E	K	I	L	L
A	D	A	M	G	S
F	C	H	A	F	T

Find the hidden words:

CAIN   KILL
ABEL   LORD
ADAM   LOVE
EVE   SIN

Place the first letter of the picture in the box.

CHILDREN'S BULLETIN

Thank God for snowflakes!

Draw a picture of something you like to do in the snow.

Winter

Every snowflake is different, just like people. That's what makes things special!

Draw some more snowflakes. Make each one different. Draw a picture of your family.

MY FAMILY

CHILDREN'S BULLETIN

Prayer

GOD WANTS US TO PRAY

Why do we end our prayer with the little word "Amen"?

Amen is like *clapping your hands.*
Amen is like *underlining* something **3 times.**
Amen is like *signing your name in big letters.*

Put an **X** by **Amen** each time you say or sing it in church today.
Put an **XX** by **Amen** each time someone else says or sings it.
Put an **!!!** by **Amen** each time you say or sing it and *really* mean it.

Amen	Amen
Amen	Amen
Amen	Amen
Amen	Amen
Amen	Amen

Our Worship should be one big Amen!

Prayer of Thanksgiving

Fill in the blanks by the picture with the word that describes the picture.

I thank you Lord for the _____
and _____ .

I thank you for the _____
and _____ .

I thank you for my _____
so warm, that keeps me safe from
wind and _____ .

I thank you for the _____
we eat.

I thank you for my _____
and _____ .

I thank you for my Savior
dear, who gives me faith and
life and cheer.   Amen!

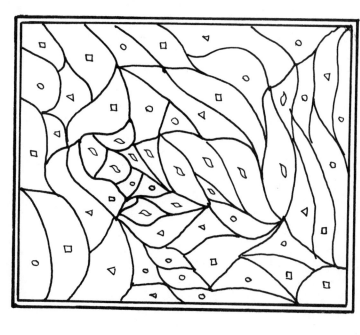

Color in the leaf spaces to see a child
praying to God.

CHILDREN'S BULLETIN

Valentine's Day

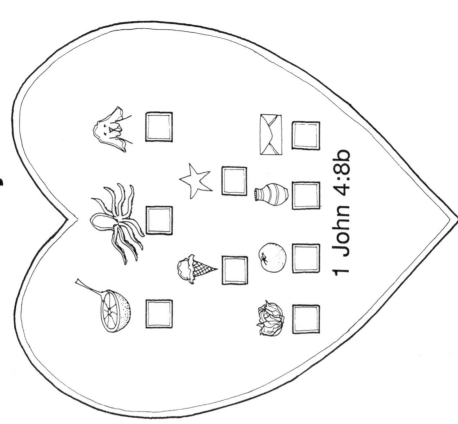

1 John 4:8b

Put the first letter of each object in the box below it.

God tells us how He wants us to love in two greatest commandments.

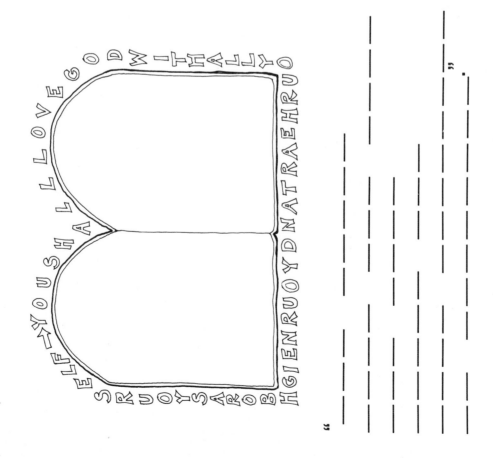

Start at the arrow and write the message on the lines below the tablets.

Valentine Match-UP

Match up the big valentine with a verse to a small one like it to see where the verse is found in the Bible.

GALATIANS 5:22

THE GREATEST OF THESE IS LOVE

MY COMMANDMENT IS THIS: LOVE EACH OTHER AS I HAVE LOVED YOU

FOR CHRIST'S LOVE COMPELS US

EPHESIANS 5:2

LIVE A LIFE OF LOVE JUST AS CHRIST LOVED US

JOHN 3:16

SERVE ONE ANOTHER IN LOVE

JOHN 15:12

GALATIANS 5:13

II CORINTHIANS 5:14

LOVE ONE ANOTHER

I JOHN 4:8B

GOD IS LOVE

ROMANS 13:8

THE FRUIT OF THE SPIRIT IS LOVE

FOR GOD LOVED THE WORLD SO

II CORINTHIANS 13:15

5

January is a good time to sit down and look back at the past and plan for the future. How do you spend your time? Discover what the Bible says about time.

Psalm 39:4

Psalm 90:12

Ephesians 5:15-17

Colossians 4:5

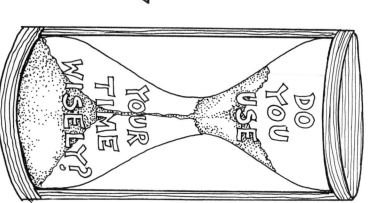

DO YOU USE YOUR TIME WISELY?

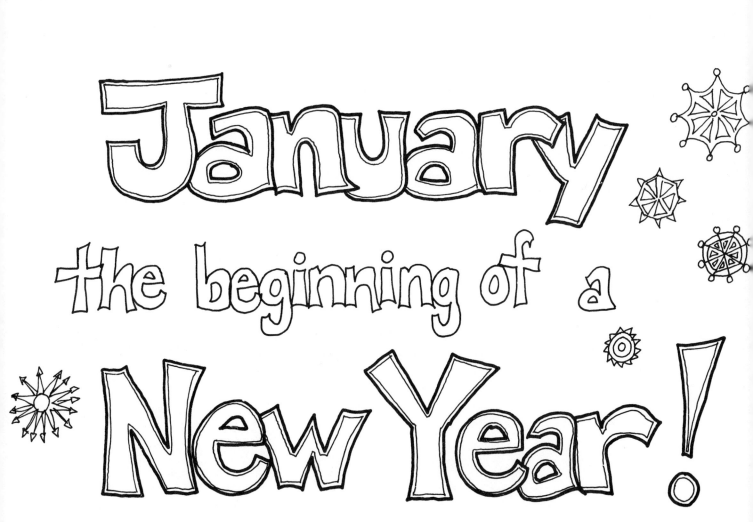

January the beginning of a New Year!

On each day in January, read a Scripture passage that tells about the boyhood of Jesus. Color a tree each time you read the daily Scripture.

Keep this in your Bible so you don't lose it.

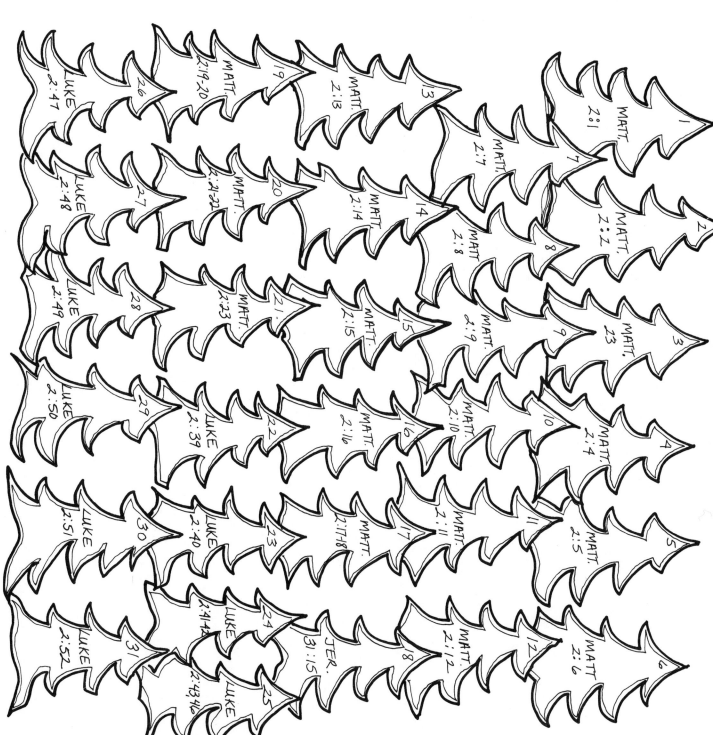

CHILDREN'S BULLETIN

New Life in Christ

GOD TURNED THIS LOWLY _____

INTO A BEAUTIFUL _____

*His love can change you too.

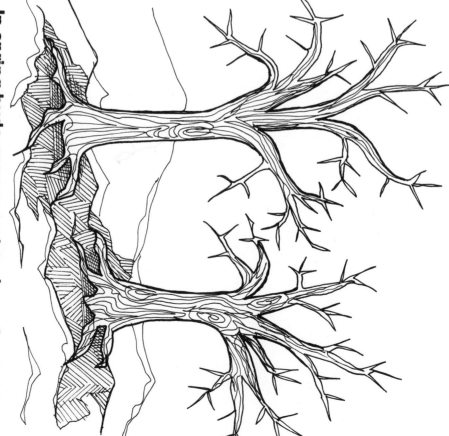

In spring buds appear on tree branches and soon they seem to spring to life again. Make these winter trees come to life with lots of leaves.

Just as a caterpillar changes into a beautiful butterfly we can have a new life in Christ. We change!

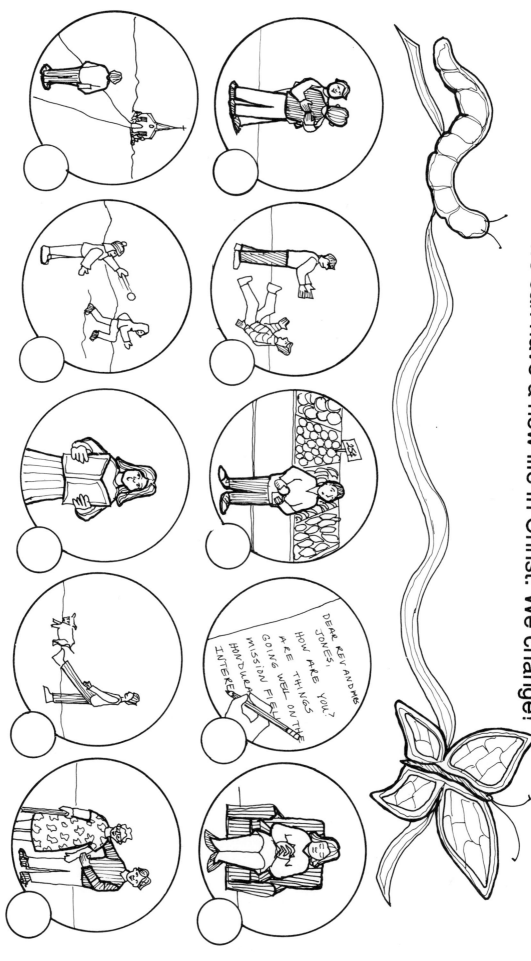

Look at each picture. Put a C (for caterpillar) in the circle if it's something we would do as our old self. Put a B (for butterfly) if it's something our new selves might do.

CHILDREN'S BULLETIN

PRESIDENT'S DAY

George W

"Honest" Abe

This week we honor George Washington and Abraham Lincoln. We remember both of them as truthful men. That's the kind of man we want for our President. Dial-a-Verse to see what God thinks of a truthful man.

Let your fingers do the walking . . .

The first # under a line tells you what # to look at on the dial. The 1, 2, or 3 tells you what letter you need in that circle on the dial. Example: 6-2=N. Get it? HAPPY DIALING!

8-1 4-2 3-2   5-3 6-3 7-2 3-1

3-1 3-2 8-1 3-2 7-3 8-1 7-3

5-3 9-3 4-3 6-2 4-1   5-3 4-3 7-1 7-3'

2-2 8-2 8-1   4-2 3-2

3-1 3-2 5-3 4-3 4-1 4-2 8-1 7-3

4-3 6-2   6-1 3-2 6-2   9-1 4-2 6-3

2-1 7-2 3-2   8-1 7-2 8-2 8-1 4-2 3-3 8-2 5-3'

Prov. 12:22

Color in letters with stars to see our hidden message.

God wants us to love and respect our leaders. Fill in the missing vowels to see what He says in Titus 3:1.

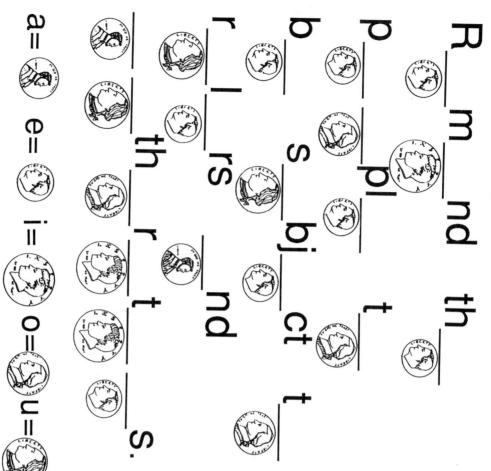

R _ m _ nd th _

p _ _ pl _ t _

b _ s _ bj _ ct t _

r _ l _ rs _ nd

th _ r _ t _ s.

a =   e =   i =   o =   u =

Each of our coins has a beautiful motto on it.

It's a tough job to be president. Remember to pray for him today and always.

Draw a picture of our president at work in the Oval Office.

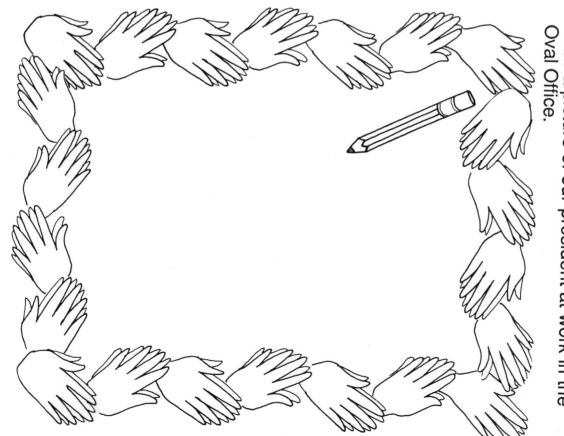

Activities and Cover Ideas

MARY, MOTHER OF JESUS

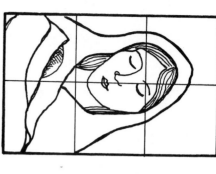

God has a plan for the world. Each of us has his or her own part in the plan. Mary's part of the plan was to be Jesus' mother. Copy this picture of Mary and Jesus into the larger grid.

Use your picture to make a Christmas card!

Advent

Many prophecies foretold the coming of the Christ. Look up the passages listed on the right and match them to the prophecies listed on the left.

"See, I will send my messenger, who will prepare the way before me."

Micah 5:2

"The scepter will not depart from Judah. . . ."

Zechariah 3:8

"A shoot will come up from the stump of Jesse. . . ."

Genesis 49:10

"But you, Bethlehem . . . out of you will come for me one who will be ruler over Israel. . . ."

Isaiah 11:1

"The stone the builders rejected has become the capstone."

Malachi 3:1

". . . I am going to bring my ser- vant the Branch. . . ."

Psalm 118:22

"For to us a child is born, to us a son is given. . . ."

Isaiah 9:6

Finish the dot-to-dot picture, and then fill in the missing letters below the picture so it tells what that special day is. The missing letters are: B, D, H, J, R, S, S, T, and Y.

_ E _ U _ ' _ _ _ _ _ A _

Hidden Words

Find these words from the scripture passage, Luke 2:8-20, hidden in other words (angel, babe, earth, glory, heaven, Joseph, Mary, praise, star).

EXAMPLE: Boys and girls can learn as they have fun.

Scan each sentence carefully . . .

1. Children listen well with each ear, the message today is for everyone.

2. A little lamb softly says, "Ba." "Be still," says its mother.

3. In time past, are you aware that when the bright light appeared to glo, Ryan sang elegently with great gladness.

4. The herdsman took his harp, raised it to his knee and plucked the strings quietly.

5. Jose, physician of the small village, is a well respected man.

6. Be careful, don't mar your new bike.

7. Heave now and move the heavy boulder.

There are some very special messengers from heaven. Through them, many people in the Bible received important news from God. You can read some stories about these helpers in Matthew 1:20-21, Luke 1:11-20, and Luke 1:26-38.

Connect the dots to find out what these messengers might have looked like.

The angels had a message for some special shepherds. To find out what it was, cross out all the odd numbers (1, 3, 5, 7, 9 are odd numbers). Put the rest of the letters in their order in the blanks.

1	2	3	6	5	7	4	9	2
A	G	E	O	T	R	O	D	
6	8	1	4	3	2	2	5	6
I	R	D	S	I	N	E	G	
4	7	8	2	7	4	3	6	2
S	M	O	F	N	T	O	H	E
7	4	5	6	3	8	1	2	1
P	S	W	A	C	V	T	I	W
2	1	4	2	5	5	8	2	
O	G	U	R	A	S	B	E	
3	2	8	5	6	7	1	5	3
E	R	T	M	H	O	E	T	D

___ ___ ___ ___ ___ ___ ,

___ ___ ___ ___ ___ ___ ___ ___ ___ !

"AND S_E BROUGHT FORTH HER
FIRS_ BORN _ON AND WRAPPED
HIM IN _WADDLING _LOTHES AND
LAD HIM IN A _ANGER;
BECAUSE THERE W_S NO _OOM
FOR THEM IN THE _NN."
LUKE 2:7

CHRISTMAS

His Name Is Wonderful

Jesus has many names.
Color in the triangles that have the following letters in them: LAMB ROOT KING
You will find a picture of another name for Jesus.
(Rev. 22:16)

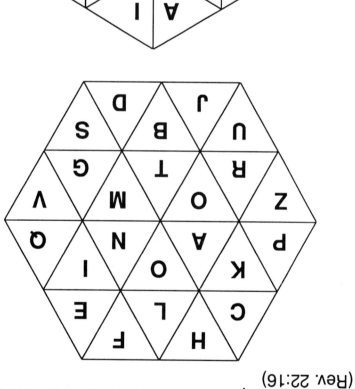

The letters in the triangles on the sides and top of the box spell out three other names for Jesus.
Each name has eight letters in it.

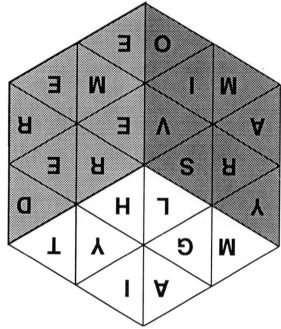

—— —— —— —— —— —— —— ——

—— —— —— —— —— —— —— ——

—— —— —— —— —— —— —— ——

```
G Q Z O A C H R I S T B K S T
O J U D E A E X R N S R B O S
D A V I D E N O S K N I E U A
P G S D R E H P E H S N T I V
E O B C N I S S F G I S R K I
E O E H B A N G E L U I O B O
N D N A R A J I H G E G T F R
Q N B E M M O R U N M N H D F
L E T M A R Y A E S D P E P I
O W N A Z A R E T H X Y D E R
R S S N M A D F N Z B O T H O
D D S G S G E O P J O S E P H
L O B E T H L E H E M O T L U
R R A R V P B O R N A R P E T
O C H I L L D V W R K L C L O M
W G A L I L E E N Y F I E L D
```

Find these words

ANGEL	GOD	SHEPHERDS
BABE	GOOD NEWS	SIGN
BETHLEHEM	INN	WORLD
BETROTHED	JOSEPH	
BORN	JOY	
CAESAR	JUDEA	
AUGUSTUS	JOY	
CHILD	LORD	
CHRIST	MANGER	
DAVID	MARY	
DECREE	NAZARETH	
FEAR	PEACE	
FIELD	PEOPLE	
GALILEE	QUIRINIUS	
GLORY	SAVIOR	

NAMES FOR JESUS

Christmas is one event that all Christians look forward to each year. Jesus' birth was something many people looked forward to for hundreds of years before he was born. The people had been told that God would send someone very special to the world.

This special person turned out to be Jesus, but there were many other names for him that showed what kind of person he would be: Emmanuel (meaning "God with us"), Messiah (meaning "The Lord's Anointed"), King, Savior, Suffering Servant, Son of Man or Son of God. Color in the shapes with dots in them and find another name people called Jesus.

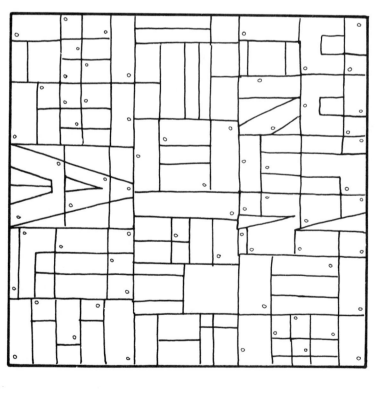

CHRISTMAS WORD PUZZLE

December—it's Christmas! So look in this rhyme for words that are hidden in letters and lines. Up, down, and crosswise, go side to side, for thirty-three words are trying to hide!

Mistletoe, holly, Nativity, star,
Gifts, bells, and swaddling, candle and cards,
Mary and Joseph, baby and manger,
Stable, poinsettia, Wise Men and shepherds,

Bethlehem, wreath, Jerusalem, carols,
Santa Claus, church, ivy and angel,
Greens, boughs, and tree, sleigh and deer,
Then chime to tell us that Christmas is here!

```
C A R O L S Y R A M E H E L H T E B
H C R U H C T G D E C E M B E R Q A
R Z L P R J I L R A N Z S H G U O B
I S J K R F V T I M N E M E S I W Y
S N L M T O I T S H E P H E R D S V
T E F S L J T M I S T L E T O E L I
M E R W R E A T H O L C A N D L E H
A R A T S A N T A C L A U S S Q I P
S G G N I N K K M A N G E R U Z G E
E M I H C G D E E R J K R Q R R H S
H O L L Y E S W A D D L I N G S E O
P R I B E L L S J S T A B L E L J K
```

CHRISTMAS CAROL CROSSWORD

1. Ring the _____
2. Once in _____ David's City
3. O Leave Your _____
4. O Come All _____ Faithful
5. Joy to the _____
6. _____ Night
7. What Can I _____ Him?
8. Away in a _____
9. Bethlehem _____ Sleeping
10. Go Tell It on the _____

Word Bank
World
Silent
Manger
Bells
Sheep
Give
Mountain
Lay
Ye
Royal

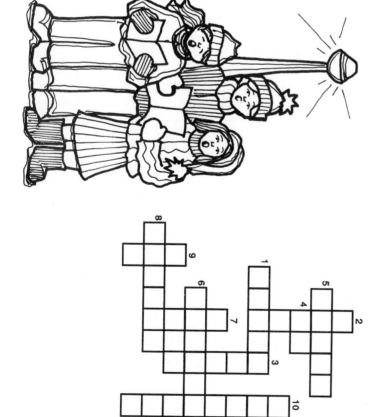

Look up John 1:9 in the Bible to complete the message.

I AM

_____

_____

Color all squares with j and x.
What is left?

_____

CHRISTMAS CROSSWORD

ACROSS

2. Jesus' first bed
7. City where Jesus was born
8. Bright light in the sky
9. Heavenly creatures who told the men of 6 DOWN of Jesus' birth

DOWN

1. One of the gifts of 4 DOWN
3. One of the gifts of 4 DOWN
4. Men who came from the east
5. One of the gifts of 4 DOWN
6. Men who were caring for flocks

EPIPHANY

Sometime after Jesus was born the wise men came, bringing gifts.

And lo, the star . . . went before them, till it came to rest over the place where the child was. When they saw the star, they rejoiced exceedingly with great joy.

Matthew 2:9–10, RSV

EMMANUEL

One of the names we call Jesus is "Emmanuel." Read Matthew 1:18-25 to find out what this word means. Now decide which path David should follow to find the right meaning of the word.

JESUS   GOD WITH US   HOLY SPIRIT

Finish this sentence:

"EMMANUEL" means _____

DRAW A SHEEP

STEP 1	STEP 2	STEP 3

Who said, "I know my sheep
and my sheep know me?"

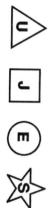

☐ ◯ ☆ △ ☆

___ ___ ___ ___ ___

Each shape stands for a letter. Write
the correct letters on the lines.

△=U ☐=J ◯=E ☆=S

JESUS CHANGES WATER
TO WINE

Unscramble
the words be-
low. They are
all taken from
Luke 2:1-11.

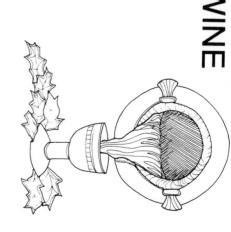

TRAWE _____

INEW _____

SUEJS _____

ACNA _____

RAYM _____

TRESNAV _____

IXS _____

NOSET _____

ARSJ _____

ARSJ _____

GWIDDEN _____

"WE HAVE FOUND THE MESSIAH!"

John 1:41

Jesus had many names. Unscramble the letters below to find names for Jesus.
Then fit the names into the puzzle.

HEARTEC	John 3:2
GINK	Luke 19:38
SESJU	Matthew 1:21
PREESDHH	John 10:14
MALE	John 1:36
AMINEMLU	Matthew 1:23
RIOVAS	John 4:42

Crossword grid with letters: M, E, S, S, I, A, H

What was Jesus' commandment to His followers? Follow the arrows in this code and finish this Bible verse:

Start Here

Code grid:
T	H
T	A
Y	O
L	U
O	V
O	E
N	E
N	A
O	T
E	H
R	A
I	S
H	A
E	V
L	O
E	V
D	Y
U	O

"This is my commandment,

____ ____ ____ ____

____ ____ ____

____ ____ ____

____ ____ ____ ____ ____

____ ____."

John 15:12

FIND A WORD

Find as many words as you can in the letters below. Go from left to right. The first one is done for you.

mangermendustarowiseastableslessing

1 manger
2 _____
3 _____
4 _____
5 _____
6 _____
7 _____
8 _____
9 _____
10 _____
11 _____
12 _____
13 _____

14 _____
15 _____
16 _____
17 _____
18 _____
19 _____
20 _____

Super Word Finder!

21 _____
22 _____
23 _____
24 _____
25 _____

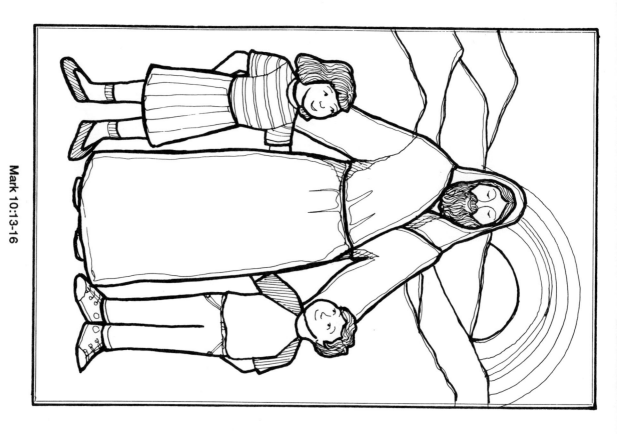

Mark 10:13-16

Jesus loves me, this I know
For the Bible tells me so.

JESUS LOVES ME

Put the key words from the beatitudes in the proper spaces in the puzzle. All the "R"'s are in place to help you.

POOR
MOURN
SPIRIT
THIRST
BLESSED
MERCIFUL
RIGHTEOUSNESS

MEEK
MERCY
HEAVEN
FILLED
INHERIT
COMFORTED

PURE
HEART
HUNGER
PEACEMAKERS
KINGDOM
PERSECUTED

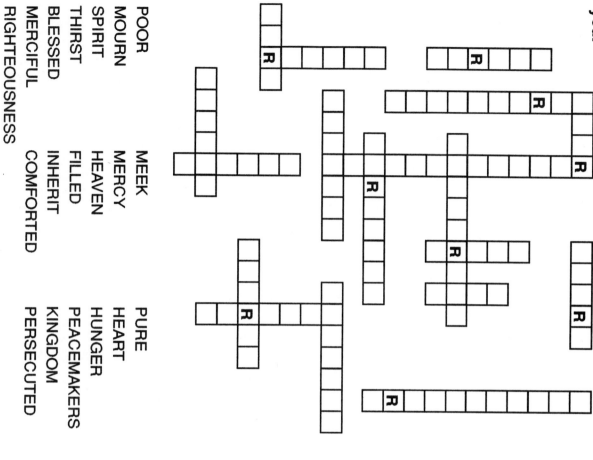

Put the first letter of the object below the line ON that line.

UNSCRAMBLE the letters in this sycomore tree and find out who is up here!

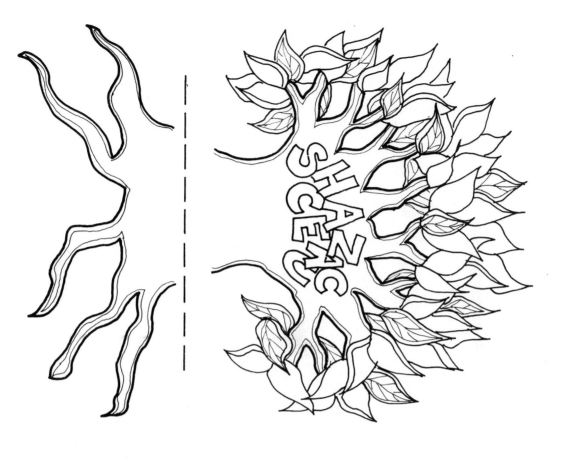

SHAZEC CEAC

If we could walk where Jesus walked . . .

Today we will take you to a few of the towns where Jesus went. He was born in B_____ in N_____. Today's message takes you to the city of J_____. It was only 18 miles from Jerusalem and 6 miles from the Jordan River. (When you get home color the countries yellow and orange; the shoreline and the seas blue.)

THINK about the miles Jesus walked in His lifetime.

Sea of Galilee

Nazareth

Jordan River

Jericho

Jerusalem

Bethlehem

Dead Sea

Fill in the letters using the code below.

Tr __5 ly __3 s __1 y t __4 y __4 __5 ,

th __2 r __3 __1 r __2 s __4 m __2

st __1 nd __3 ng h __2 r __2 wh __4 w __3 ll

n __1 t t __3 st d __2 __1 th b __2 f __4 r __2

th __2 y s __2 __2 th __1 t th __2

k __3 ngd __4 m __4 f G __4 d h __1 s

c __4 m __2 w __3 th p __4 w __2 r.

M __1 rk 9:1

a = 1   e = 2   i = 3

o = 4   u = 5

Transfiguration Word Search

Find these words from Mark 9:1-8:

Jesus, Peter, James, John, Elijah, Moses, mountain, white, cloud, voice, shelters, son, love, enveloped, alone

```
B P Q S V O I C E F
T E S R E T L E H S
G E V O N Y L I W M
A R J S V B O Y A O
P D H E W E U C I U
K E A S D Z D V A N
P P W C K J P L J T
J O H E G L O R Y A
A L I M R N F H X I
M E T N E Y R K N N
E V E L I J A H N P
S N K I N G D O M S
O E Z C J E S U S M
```

Draw pictures of four needs you might pray for.

Connect the dots in each square.

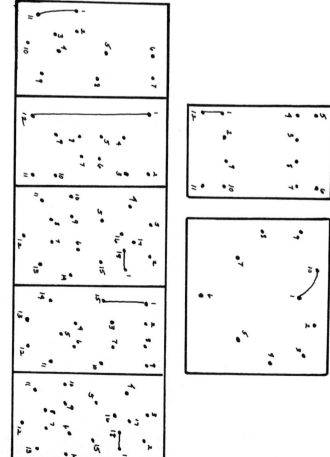

Now draw a picture of a happy boy or girl.

G   I   H

L   F   T

M   E   D

A   O   W

R

Use the code to find out what Jesus said about Himself. Then read John 8:12.

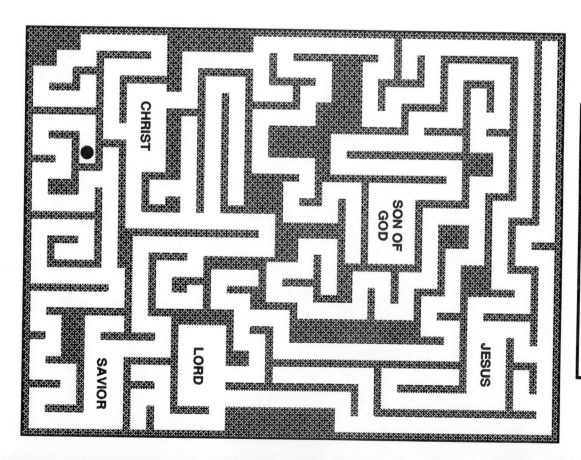

Start at the dot and find the five names of Jesus.

CHRIST

SON OF GOD

JESUS

LORD

SAVIOR

FAITH IN JESUS

DESIGN YOUR OWN CROSS

The Cross is the most popular symbol of the Christian faith. It has been used by Christians through the ages to remind us of how Jesus brought us life through death on a cross. There are many different kinds of crosses. Below are four samples.

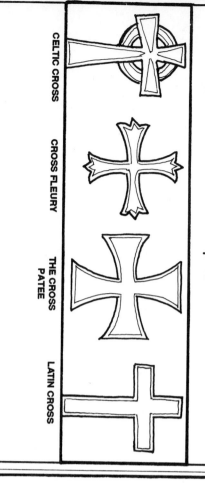

CELTIC CROSS   CROSS FLEURY   THE CROSS PATEE   LATIN CROSS

Use the space above to design a cross.

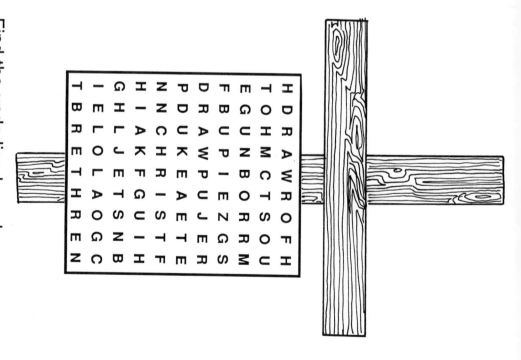

Find the underlined words

"<u>Brethren</u>, I do not consider that I have made it my own; but one thing I do, <u>forgetting</u> what lies <u>behind</u> and straining <u>forward</u> to what lies ahead, I press on toward the <u>goal</u> for the prize of the <u>upward</u> <u>call</u> of <u>God</u> in <u>Christ Jesus</u>."

Philippians 3:13-14 (RSV)

```
H D A W R O F H
T O H M C T S O U
E G U N B O R R M
F B U P I E Z G S
D R A W P U J E R
P D U K E A E T E
N N C H R I S T F
H I A K F G U I H
G H L J E T S N B
I E L O L A O G C
T B R E T H R E N
```

THE TEN COMMAMANDMENTS

1
You shall have no other _____ before me.

2
You shall not _____ for yourself an _____.

3
You shall not misuse the _____ of the _____ your God.

4
Remember the _____ day by keeping it _____.

5
Honor your _____ and your _____.

6
You shall not _____.

7
You shall not commit _____.

8
You shall not _____.

9
You shall not give false _____ against your _____.

10
You shall not _____ your neighbor's _____. You shall not covet your neighbor's wife, or his _____ or maidservant, his _____ or donkey, or anything that belongs to your _____.

Exodus 20:3-17 (NIV)

GOD'S RULES FOR US

This is number ____

Do not ___ ___ ___ ___ ___ ___ ___ ___ ___ ___ ___ ___ ___
      40   36 12   i   24 16

of ___ ___a___ ___i___ that
  12   a 44 32   i 24 8   to get

___e___ ___o___ ___ to
36 e 20   o 24 8   32

o___ ___ ___e___ ___ .
o 36 12   e 28 32

Each number stands for a letter. Write the letters in the spaces.

4 = b	28 = r
8 = g	32 = s
12 = h	36 = t
16 = k	40 = w
20 = l	44 = y
24 = n	

Jesus gave us two important command-ments. Read them to yourself. Then find the underlined words in the square.

"<u>Love</u> the <u>Lord</u> with all your <u>heart</u>, with all your <u>soul</u>, with all your <u>mind</u>, and with all your <u>strength</u>.
The <u>second</u> most important <u>command-ment</u> is this: Love your <u>neighbor</u> as you love <u>yourself</u>."

Mark 12:30-31

```
I X S E C O N D Q U E K
M N L S Z G O D F Z T F
P E Q O F D N I M N L L
O I U V Z U E E X Z E E
R G Z L Y E G M G A Q S
T H H J Z F D X L L V R
A B R E K N Q J O L I U
N O G D A X Q N R N K O
T R L M K R X L D T Q Y
P Z M D Q J T F Z G Z X
Q O R X S T R E N G T H
C B Q E E H Q Z X K J H
```

God gave us 10 rules.
This is number ____.

GOD'S RULES FOR US

Write the alphabet letter that comes before each letter.

Do not | i | s | n | another with what you

| t | a | | a | z | ; be he your

buddy or | t | p | n | f | p | o | f | | c | f | t | u |

not | m | j | l | f | you. | H | f | m | q | who does

others to | l | f | f | q | their | h | p | p | e |

names. Say only the | c | f | t | u | about

| f | w | f | s | z | p | o | f | .

Draw a <u>sad</u> face

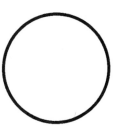

This is how we feel when we don't obey God's law.

Unscramble the letters to find out the feelings that complete the thought . . . .

I am sad when I . . . .

1. tuhr
2. ehcta
3. eli
4. (am) ljeosua
5. ehta
6. (have no) hfita
7. (do not) yboe
8. (am) degeyr

_____
_____
_____
_____
_____

Draw a <u>happy</u> face

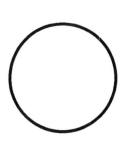

This is how we feel when Jesus for-gives our sins.

A Matter of Life and Death

Philippians 1:21

Q. What is your only comfort?

A. That I belong to Jesus and He loves and cares for me as a good shepherd cares for his sheep.

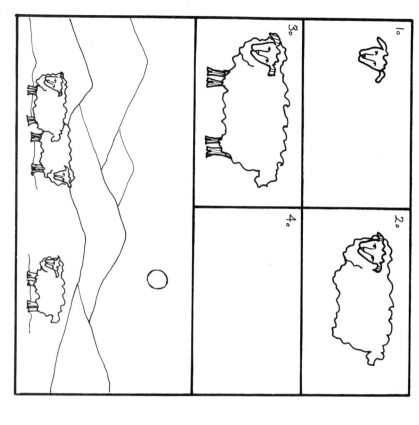

Follow the steps in each box. Draw your sheep in Box #4.

THE THREE FACES OF GOD

FATHER

GOD

SON

HOLY SPIRIT

How well do you know your math? Does **3=1**? It *does* if you're talking about the . . .

S Q H M H S X

Look at the letter under the line. Write the next letter in the alphabet on the line.

Q. What is true faith?

A. Start at the **K** and write down every other letter to see what true faith is.

TRUE FAITH IS:

_____

_____

_____

_____

K @ N S @ U W R E N M G Y T S H A N T S H A R E B E E F O H B R L @ E E H Y S E T N @ R U and

How Does God
Show Us His Will?

The letters below form one sentence, but there is one bad letter which has squeezed in between the other letters to mess up the message. Find that letter and cross it out wherever you find it. Then you will be able to read the hidden sentence. Write it on the lines below.

A V E C R C Y
I M C P O R T C A N C T
B O C O K I S C G O D ' S
C H O L C Y W O R C D ,
T C H E B I C B L E .

_____

_____

_____

Q. Did God create us so sinful?
A. No!! We were created in . . .

God made us perfect. . . . . We blew it! Here is a picture to remind us of the story of creation and the fall.

GOD'S IMAGE

Look at the letters in the *reflection*. Make the real letter above each line to see how we were created.

Q. How did we become so evil?
A. God created man good—a real

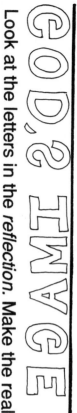

_____ _____

but, when Adam & Eve sinned in the Garden of Eden, man became like a

_____ _____

Fill in the missing letters to find some colorful terms. Ask your folks what they mean.

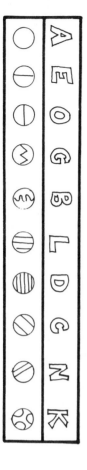

A	E	O	G	B	L	D	C	N	K

Q. How can we escape punishment and be right with God?

A. Only after the **debt** is **paid**.

Q. Can we pay this debt ourselves?

A. No!! We, as **sinners**, just make it **worse** each **day**.

Q. Can another creature pay the debt for us?

A. No!! **God** would not **punish** another **creature** for **man**'s sins. Besides that wouldn't be **payment** enough.

Q. Who then could pay for our sins (or be our mediator)? [A mediator is someone who goes between two things—like a bridge.]

A. Only **someone who** is **both human** and God.

Q. Who is our mediator?

A. To see who it would be, color the open path in the maze as you go along. Don't cross any lines but color in every open path you come to. It's started for you. The name of our mediator will show up in the maze.

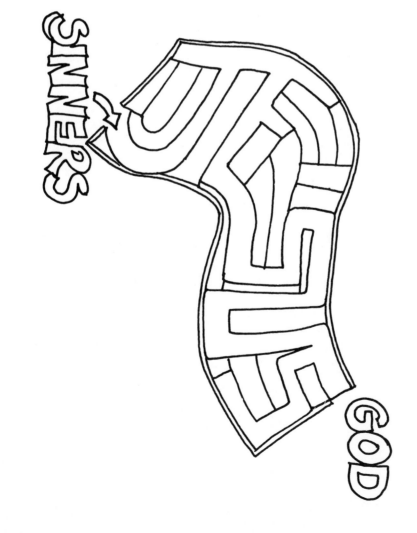

Word Search

```
V C F Y A D E B T C G
S R E N N I S H J R I
A H O K W A R G L E M
S U N E H P O O U A B
Q M L M O D W Y N T O
R A Y P U N I S H U T
T N T N E M Y A P R H
O S O M E O N E F E F
```

Find all of the **darkened** words in the Word Search.

Q. If there is only one God, why do we talk about three?

A. If you have faith in the *true* God, you believe in God the Father, God the Son, and God the Holy Spirit.

Here is 1 apple. The apple has 3 parts.

$\overline{16}\ \overline{5}\ \overline{5}\ \overline{12}$ $\overline{6}\ \overline{12}\ \overline{5}\ \overline{19}\ \overline{8}$ $\overline{3}\ \overline{15}\ \overline{18}\ \overline{5}$

The 3 parts of the apple have different purposes:

The peel $\overline{16}\ \overline{18}\ \overline{15}\ \overline{20}\ \overline{5}\ \overline{3}\ \overline{20}\ \overline{19}$.

It keeps the apple healthy.

The flesh of the apple is good to

$\overline{5}\ \overline{1}\ \overline{20}$.

The core of the apple contains

$\overline{19}\ \overline{5}\ \overline{5}\ \overline{4}\ \overline{19}$ from which apple trees

grow.

THE APPLE HAS 3 PARTS BUT YOU KNOW
YOU DON'T HAVE 3 APPLES—JUST 1.

A	B	C	D	E	F	G	H	I	J	K	L	M
1	2	3	4	5	6	7	8	9	10	11	12	13

N	O	P	Q	R	S	T	U	V	W	X	Y	Z
14	15	16	17	18	19	20	21	22	23	24	25	26

THERE IS ONLY 1 TRUE GOD.

The 1 true God has 3 persons:
GOD THE FATHER,
GOD THE SON, and
GOD THE HOLY SPIRIT

The 3 persons of the 1 true God have different purposes.

God the Father is our $\overline{3}\ \overline{18}\ \overline{5}\ \overline{1}\ \overline{20}\ \overline{15}\ \overline{18}$.

God the Son is our $\overline{19}\ \overline{1}\ \overline{22}\ \overline{9}\ \overline{15}\ \overline{18}$.

God the Holy Spirit makes us $\overline{8}\ \overline{15}\ \overline{12}\ \overline{25}$.

The **3 main ways we can know God is** 🕊 **the Father,** ✝ **the Son, and** 🕊 **the Holy Spirit.**

Find 3 of each of these symbols in the picture.

PUT ON THE FULL ARMOR OF GOD

Below is a list of the spiritual weapons that God has given us. Can you put each one in its correct place on the man of armor on the opposite page?

Truth

Righteousness

The gospel of peace

Faith

Salvation

The Spirit, which is the Word of God

(Answer: Ephesians 6:14-18)

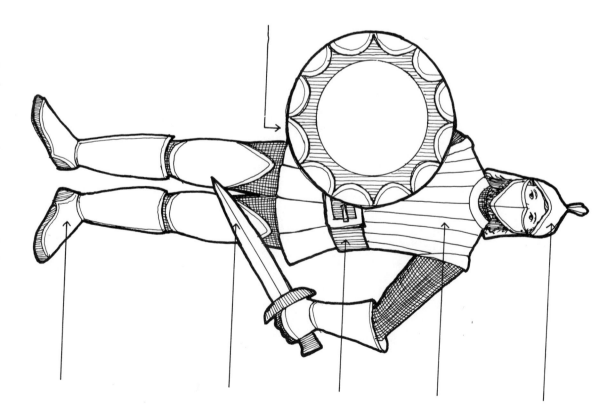

STAND FIRM THEN!

Remember Who You Are

Isaiah 49:1

We Are God's Covenant People

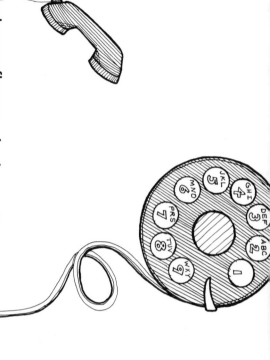

Look at your fingertips. Do you see anything? Are they smooth? If you put ink on one and pressed it on a piece of paper, you would see many little lines. This is called a fingerprint. You can't see them, but fingerprints identify us.

God's people have something that identify them, too. They have been baptized with *water* to identify them as God's covenant people.

Can you make these fingerprints into some *covenant people*?

Use these prints to make some interesting creatures.

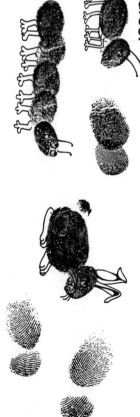

Let your fingers do the walking . . .

The first # under a line tells you what # to look at on the dial. The 1, 2, or 3 tells you what letter you need in that circle on the dial. Example: 6-2=N. Get it? HAPPY DIALING!

Providence means

4-1	6-3	3-1

7-1	7-2	6-3	8-3	4-3	3-1	3-2	7-3

The butterfly is a sign of new life. It changes from a caterpillar to a butterfly through a beautiful plan of God. Saul changed from a sinner to a saint through the grace of God and so can we! Draw a butterfly to remind you of that.

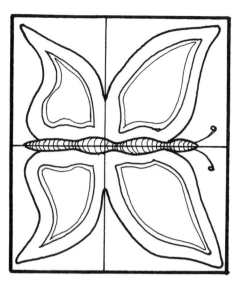

Q. Is it fair that God ask us to be perfect when it's impossible for us?

A. Line 1 **Y E S O N E B E C A U S E F O U R H E**
Line 2 **M A D E Y E S U S N O P E R F E C T**
Line 3 **S O U L M A N R U I N E D I T B O D Y**
Line 4 **R E D W H E N B L U E A D A M G O L D**
Line 5 **A B C S A I B N C N A E B D C A B C A**

Our sins *must* be paid for!

To find our answer follow these instructions:

Cross out the 2 *number* words in Line 1.
Cross out the *answer* words in Line 2. (Yes/No)
Cross out the first four and the last four letters in Line 3.
Cross out the 3 *color* words in Line 4.
Cross out all of the *A's, B's & C's* in Line 5.

Q. Will God let sin go unpunished?
A. No! Dial-a-Verse to see what Paul tells us in Romans 6:23.

| 3-3 | 6-3 | 7-2 | | 8-1 | 4-2 | 3-2 | | 9-1 | 2-1 | 4-1 | 3-2 | 7-3 |

| 6-3 | 3-3 | | 3-1 | 3-2 | 2-1 | 8-1 | 4-2 |

| 7-3 | 4-3 | 6-2 | 4-3 | 7-3 |

Let your fingers do the walking . . .

The first # under a line tells you what # to look at on the dial. The 1, 2, or 3 tells you what letter you need in that circle on the dial. Example: 6-2=N. Get it? HAPPY DIALING!

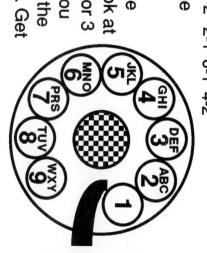

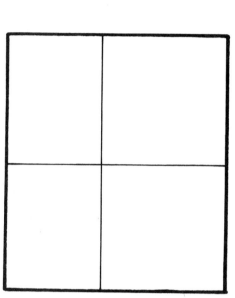

CHILDREN'S BULLETIN

This morning in church we will sing the song "Holy, Holy, Holy." When we say the God is holy it means that He is perfect and pure and that we should worship Him.

In Church today we will do many things to help us worship God.

Count the number of songs we sing.

Count the number of times we pray. _____

How many times do we or someone else read the Bible? _____

How many songs does the Choir sing? _____

What book of the Bible does the pastor preach from? _____

What is the title of his sermon? _____

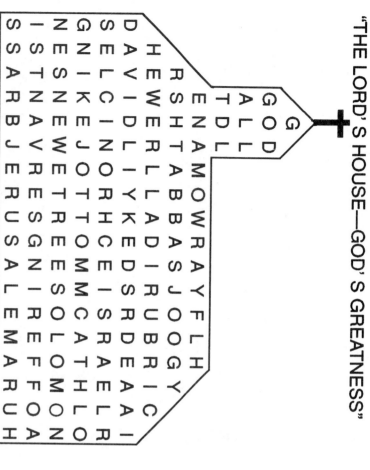

```
        G O D
        A L L
        T D L
E N A M O W R A Y F L H
R S H T A B B A S J O O G Y
H E W E R L L A D I R U B R I C
S E L C I N O R H C E I S R A E L
D A V I D L I Y K E D S R D E A A I
G N I K E J O T T O M M C A T H L O
N E S N E W E T R E E S O L O M O N
I S T N A V R E S G N I R E F F O A
S S A R B J E R U S A L E M A R U H
```

ALL
BRASS
CEDAR
CHRONICLES
DAVID
FOURSCORE
GATES
GEMS
GOD
GOLD
GREAT
HEWER

HOUSE
HURAM
IRON
ISRAEL
JERUSALEM
JOY
JUDAH
KING
LINEN
LORD
MEN

OIL
RUBRIC
SABBATHS
SERVANTS
SILVER
SINGS
SKILL
SOLOMON
TREES
WOMAN
WORK

A-MAZING HEART puzzle . . .
"Put God's word in your heart!"

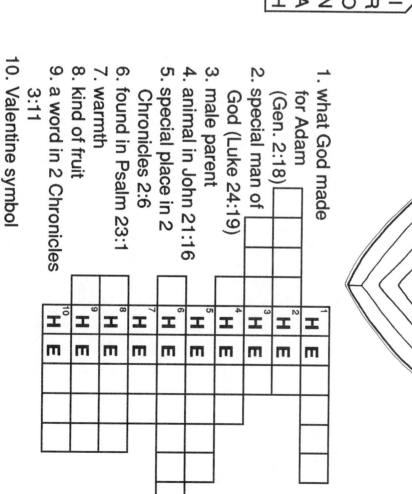

1. what God made for Adam (Gen. 2:18)
2. special man of God (Luke 24:19)
3. male parent
4. animal in John 21:16
5. special place in 2 Chronicles 2:6
6. found in Psalm 23:1
7. warmth
8. kind of fruit
9. a word in 2 Chronicles 3:11
10. Valentine symbol

Be a Good Neighbor

Fill in this verse:

" _____ your _____

as yourself. " Luke 10:27

List four ways you can be a good
neighbor:

1. _____

2. _____

3. _____

4. _____

PUT CHRIST FIRST
IN YOUR LIFE

Fill in the squares under each letter in
CHRIST by using these clues:

C - where you worship

H - where you live

R - play time at school

I - a measure on a ruler

S - where you study and learn

T - what you do when you go on a trip

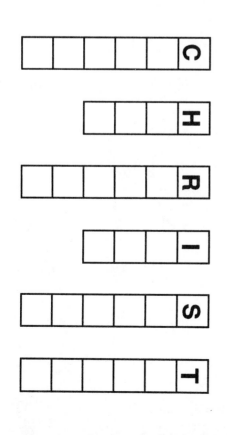

The sermon this morning is about Noah. God was unhappy with all the sin in the world, so He decided to send a flood. He saw that Noah was a good man. God told Noah to build a huge boat and to put 2 of every kind of animal in it. People laughed at Noah, but Noah trusted God. He knew that God would take care of his family. We, too, must trust that God knows what's best for us, and that He will take care of us.

Find 10 animals hiding from Noah. Then color the picture.

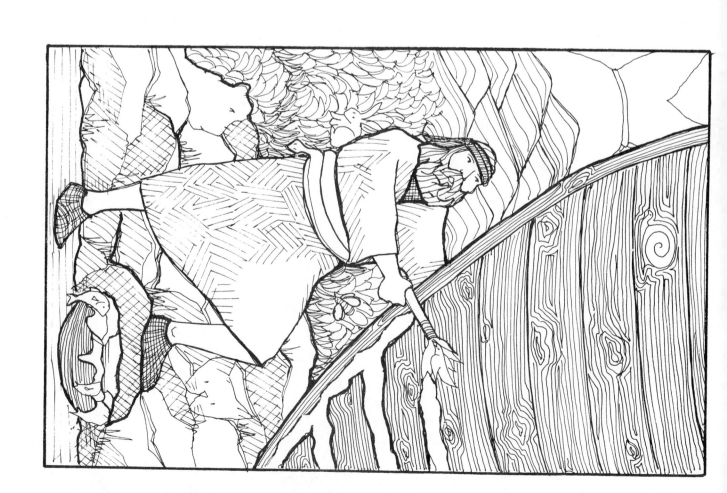

Put one letter in each box to finish this puzzle. The passages are all from Genesis.

1. Joseph's father (49:29)
2. Joseph had a beautiful _____ (37:3).
3. There were _____ years of prosperity and _____ years of famine (41:29-30).
4. Joseph interpreted the cupbearer's and the _____'s dream (40:16).
5. He made Joseph second-in-command of all Egypt (41:39-40).
6. He was Joseph's first master (39:1).

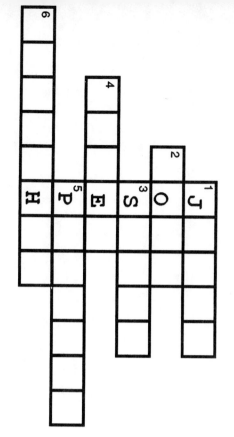

A W N A D
F
E
T
M
C

God said,

E
E
R F O R F E

Start at the **W** and write down every other letter to see our verse from Genesis 17. Color in the picture of Abraham.

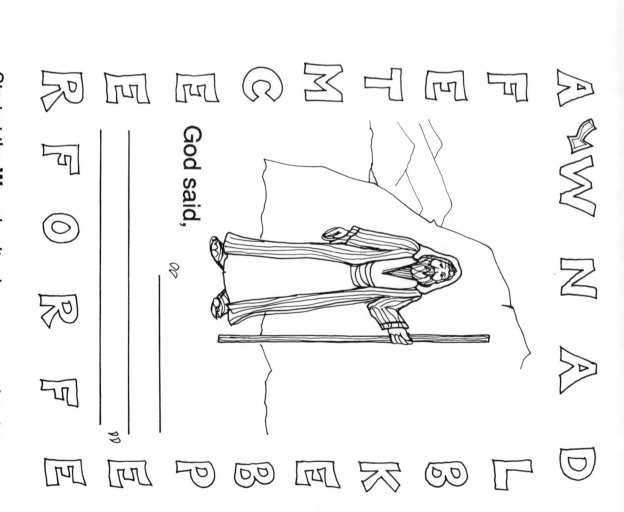

L
B
K
E
B
P
E
F

Daniel and the Feast of Belshazzar

Daniel 5

King Belshazzar made a great feast.
Many people came to the feast.
They drank wine from the gold cups that had come from God's temple in
Jerusalem.
They drank wine and praised false gods.
Then a hand was seen writing a message on the wall.
Daniel was able to tell the meaning of the message.
King Belshazzar did not fear God.
That night he died.

Using the key above, decipher the coded message below.

DANIEL IN THE LIONS' DEN

Daniel 6

Below is a one-way crossword puzzle to solve. All the clues are in verse 10. Write the answers in the verse below and then in the puzzle squares.

1
2
3
4
5
6

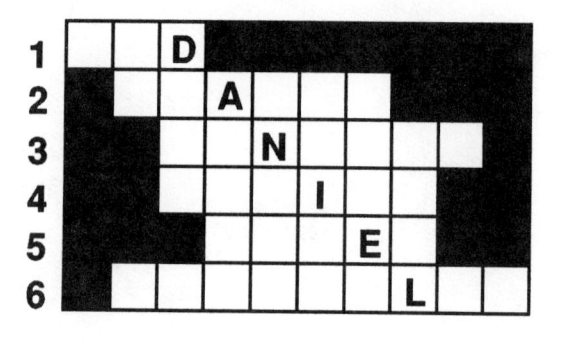

"Now when (4)__________ learned that the decree had been published, he went home to his upstairs room where the (3)__________ opened toward (6)__________. (5)__________ times a day, he got down on his knees and (2)__________, giving thanks to his (1)__________ just as he had done before."

The answers to this part are found in verses 21 and 22.

1
2
3
4
5
6
7
8

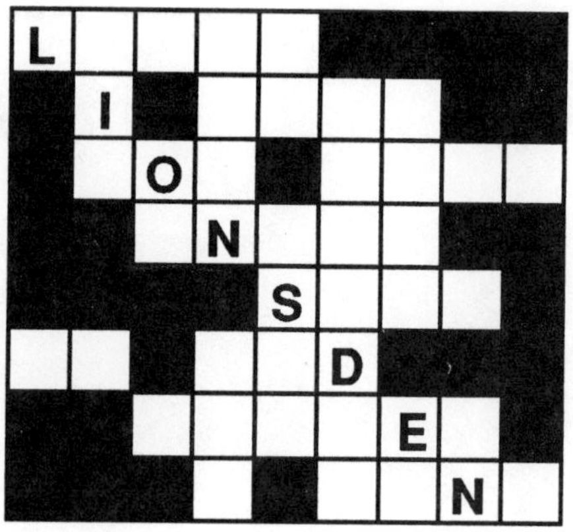

(7)"__________ answered, (8)'__ ________, live forever! (6)__________sent his (4)__________, and he (5)__________ the mouths of the (1)__________. That they have (3)___ ______ me, because I was found innocent in his sight. Nor have (2)__ ever _______ any wrong before you, O king.'"

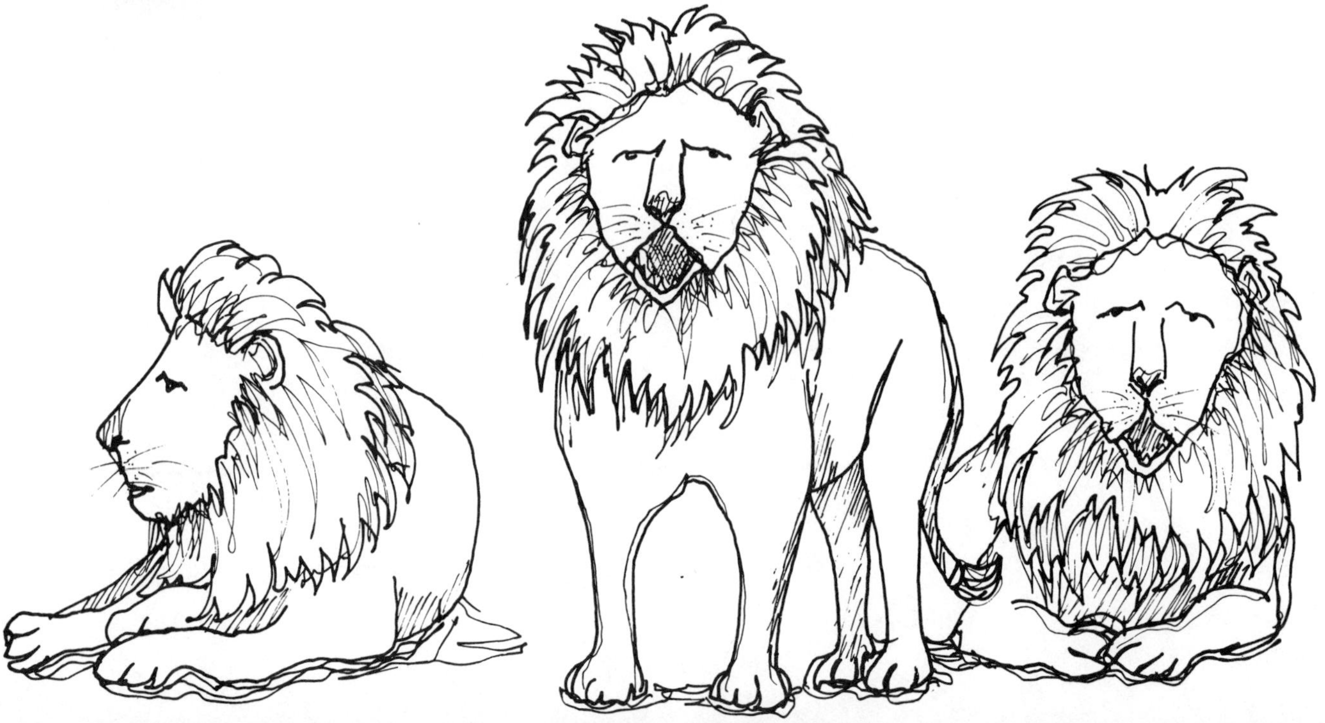

Use this telephone dial to complete the verse below. The code is used by first dialing the numbers, then dialing the letter in that circle. For example: 22 is circle number two and the second letter in that circle, "B"; 71 is circle number seven and the first letter in that circle, "P."

22-32-53-43-32-83-32   43-62   81-42-32   53-63-72-31

B_____   _____   _____   _____

51-32-73-82-73   21-62-31   93-63-82   91-43-53-53   22-32

_____   _____   _____   _____   _____

73-21-83-32-31   93-63-82   21-62-3193-63-82-72

_____   _____   _____

42-63-82-73-32-42-63-53-31   21-23-81-73

_____   _____ **16:31**

GOD'S PROMISE

God has promised that season shall always follow season. Read that promise in Gen. 8:22, then try to find all the words of the promise in the word search below. Words found more than one time in the text are used only one time in the puzzle.

```
D T J X B S S K I H W G N O C Y
W Z A Q J I U M C X D A S K Q E
J C Z J Q U M R C C T Y C O L G
J J M C A K M V B E A R T H P X
N T Z N E V E R W A N H N T L M
R G A I H A R V E S T E O O C T
L O N G A S H T H E N D U R E S
G D D H I W I N T E R A K A P P
H E A T P G C O L D Y Y O X G M
G X N B K D M R D T B X Z E D X
J V Z C A H B R W I L L G H G K
O L Q W S I Z D B M H D A D D R
Z M Q I D D Q J H E H A J K C S
```

Can you find these words?

AND	EARTH	NEVER	WILL
AS	ENDURES	NIGHT	WINTER
CEASE	HARVEST	SEEDTIME	
COLD	HEAT	SUMMER	
DAY	LONG	THE	

WORD SEARCH

receiving	giving	heart	
God	time	offering	
myself	deacon	tithe	
cheerful	stewardship		

```
A B C D C H E E R F U L C
E G O D L M P S T U V R D
F H F J H N Q W X Y Z E E
G I F K E O R A B T M C F
S T E W A R D S H I P E G
H I R J R K L M T T N I O
W V I U T T N S R H Q V P
X Y N Z A O B T C E D I E
F G G H C I J K N O P N Q
R S T A L M G I V I N G F
U V E W X Y Z A B C D E G
H D M Y S E L F I J K L M
```

HIDDEN NAMES

EXAMPLE: Ada made a speech to the crowd

(If you need help, the answers are on the bottom of the next page.)

1. Dynamo sessions begin at two o'clock.   ___ In host but not hot

2. Please—No Children Allowed!   ___ In sheep but not sleep

3. Give me the simple life!   ___ In peace but not pack

4. The boa zipped through the grass.   ___ In praise but not raise

5. Nonalcoholic ale beats turpentine for remov-   ___ In Esther but not Easter
   ing paint.

6. Use a sack for a Halloween mask.   ___ In babe but not baby

7. The clever lad amused the king with his   ___ In country but not county
   magical tricks.

8. The party started with the sound of a bell.   ___ In heard but not heart

9. Nothing is as pesky as a mosquito.   ___ In haste but not hate

10. The motel is half full tonight.

> Think of some other people in the Bible and make
> your own HIDDEN NAME sentences.

Answers:
1. Moses/Amos 2. Enoch 3. Eli 4. Boaz 5. Caleb
6. Asa 7. Adam/Eve 8. Abel 9. Asa/Amos 10. Elisha

Find a letter in the first underlined word that is not in the second one, fill in the blanks, and find some key people in today's message!

STACK-A-WORD*
2 Kings 7:1–20

ACROSS

Camp
Elisha
Four
Measure
Shekels
Syrians

UP & DOWN

Barley
Famine
Kings
Lepers
Prophecy
Samaria
Tents

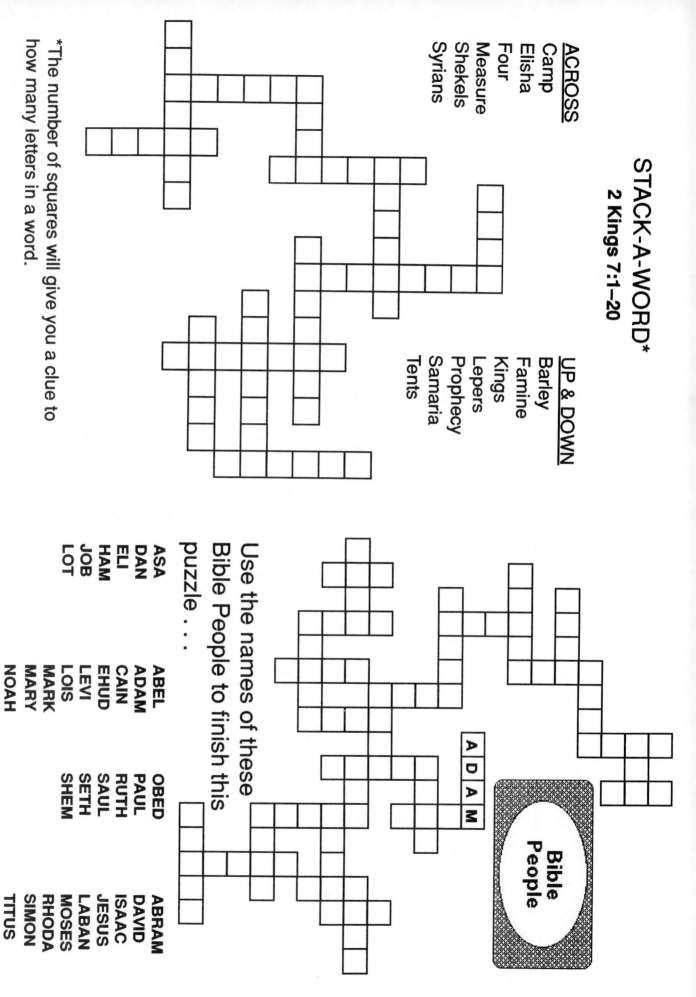

Use the names of these Bible People to finish this puzzle . . . .

Bible People

ABEL
ADAM
CAIN
EHUD
LEVI
LOIS
MARK
MARY
NOAH
SHEM

ASA
DAN
ELI
HAM
JOB
LOT

OBED
PAUL
RUTH
SAUL
SETH
SHEM

ABRAM
DAVID
ISAAC
JESUS
LABAN
MOSES
RHODA
SIMON
TITUS

A D A M

*The number of squares will give you a clue to how many letters in a word.

Trust God with tomorrow · Help someone today

GIVE ME FIVE!

Write the name of a Bible character whose name starts with each of these first five letters of the alphabet.

A _____

B _____

C _____

D _____

E _____

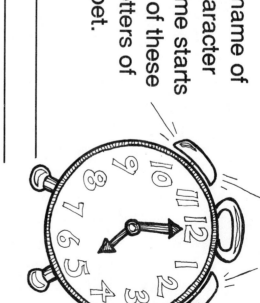

Name 5 books of the Old Testament.

1. _____

2. _____

3. _____

4. _____

5. _____

Below is a verse about trusting in God. Fill in the missing letters in the words by matching the shapes of the boxes.

TR⬡ST ⬦N TH⬡ L⬦RD W⬡TH ⬡LL TH⬡N⬜ H⬦⬡RT

Proverbs 3:5

⬡ A   ⬡ E   ⬦ I   ⬜ O   △ U

EASTER

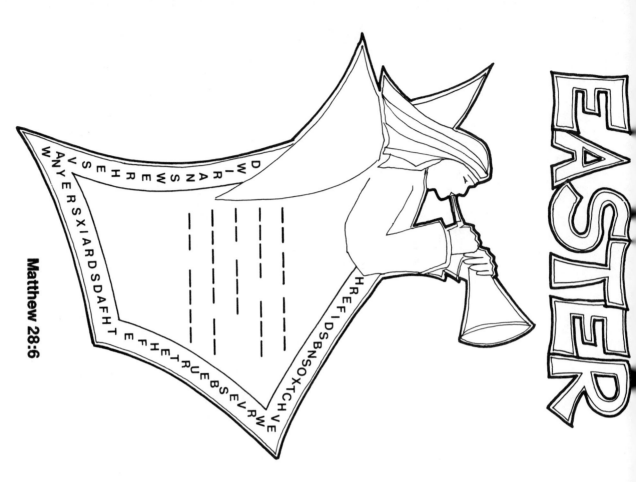

Matthew 28:6

Code: To find the angel's Easter message to the women, start at the 'H' and write down every other letter.

Color in the letters with ○ in them.

LABOR DAY

WORKERS OF AMERICA

Stand up and take a bow!

Can you identify each of these laborers? Whatever you are called upon to do in this life, God wants you to do your very *BEST* so that He may be glorified.

Match up the person from our church with his or her work

Banker _____

Teacher _____

Dentist _____

Operate Greenhouses _____

Church Secretary _____

Policeman _____

Truck driver _____

Bus driver _____

Store owner _____

Mechanic _____

CHILDREN'S BULLETIN

God Sent His _____ !

Draw-in Pictures

A robin is a sign
of spring.
Give him a bill so
he can sing.

Through the air this
kite will sail,
If you will add a
fancy tail.

Draw one curved line,
If you would try.
To help keep someone
nice and dry.

Into the garden
fall spring showers.
Would you like to
draw the flowers?

CHILDREN'S BULLETIN

ADVENT

SECOND WEEK:

Why do we light 2 candles?

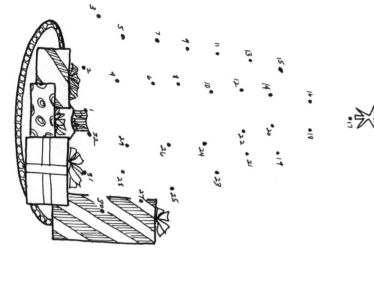

Last week we learned that the 1st candle stood for Christ—the Light of the World. Today we see that the 2nd candle stands for the great gift that God gives us—His Son.

This dot-to-dot will help you remember both of them. The star can stand for **Christ—the light of the world.** The *gift* under the tree can stand for **God's Great Gift.**

Hidden Tulips

Find and color the twelve tulips hidden in the stained glass window.

Do you see a hidden word?

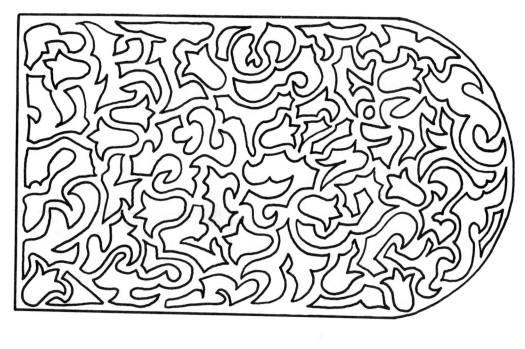

CHILDREN'S BULLETIN

Fill in this verse:

"—— —— shall —— ——
the Lord your —— and
—— only shall you
—— —— —— ——"
Matthew 4:10

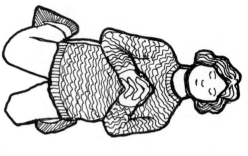

RUN THE RACE!

HELP THIS RUNNER TO THE FINISH LINE

FINISH

A DOLLAR AND A CENT

A big silver dollar and a
little brown cent

Paste a new penny here

Rolling along together they went.
Rolling along the smooth sidewalk,
When the dollar remarked, for dollars
do talk,
"You poor little cent, you cheap little
mite,
I am bigger and twice as bright;
I'm worth more than you a hundredfold,
And written on me in letter bold-
Is the motto drawn from a pious creed,
'In God We Trust,' which all may read."
"Yes, I know," said the cent, "I'm a
cheap little mite.
And I know I'm not big nor bright.
And yet," said the cent with a meek
little sigh,
"You don't go to church as often as I."

"CARE FOR THE CHILDREN"

From the word LIFE to the word GIFT:
change only ONE letter each word
and work down the list to GIFT

1. to be alive   1. ___ LIFE
2. to have life is to   2. _ _ _ _
3. I John 4:19 "We   3. _ _ _ _
   ___ him . . ."
4. only one   4. _ _ _ _
5. the phone has a   5. _ _ _ _
   dial ___
6. part of a fork   6. _ _ _ _
7. a light coloring   7. _ _ _ _
8. fuzz from clothes   8. _ _ _ _
9. to raise upward   9. _ _ _ _
10. another word for a   10. ___ GIFT
    present

(these will be all four letter words)

"Life is a gift"

Answers:

1. Life2. Live3. Love4. Lone5. Tone
6. Tine 7. Tint8. Lint9. Lift10. Gift

SHARING JESUS

Who needs to hear the Good News about Jesus? Find and circle the faces hidden in this picture.

Many of God's children look different and have different customs than we have. Jesus loves children and wants them to know about Him.

When we read the Bible verse of All Nations Heritage Week, we realize that God loves **all** kinds of people. The words of a children's song remind us of that.

Jesus loves the little children
All the children of the world
Red and yellow, black and white,
They are precious in His sight
Jesus loves the little children of the world.

You [Christ] bought us for God of every race, language, people and nation . . .

Revelation 5:9b

Find all of the words to this special song in the Word Search.
(Each word is there once.)

G	H	T	K	C	A	L	B
Y	F	C	D	N	A	L	L
E	W	H	I	T	E	O	O
L	R	I	N	A	H	F	V
L	E	L	I	T	T	L	E
E	D	D	J	E	S	U	S
W	O	R	L	D	H	I	S
T	H	E	Y	E	R	A	F
Y	E	N	S	I	G	H	T
S	U	O	I	C	E	R	P

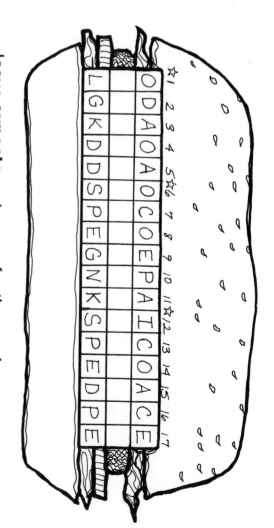

Jesus **expects** us to care for those who are poor and hungry. This sandwich can remind us of that.

Look at the pictures below so you can guess which missing letter will complete the three-letter sandwich words. The *filling* in the sandwich will tell you what special day we are observing today.

When you see a ☆ before a number, capitalize the letter you write.

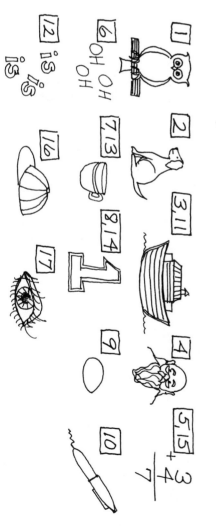

Jesus taught us to pray.

Find 10 pairs of praying hands
hidden in picture.

Our Father in heaven,
hallowed be your name,
your kingdom come,
your will be done
    on earth as it is in heaven.
Give us today our daily bread.
Forgive us our debts,
    as we also have forgiven our debtors.
And lead us not into temptation,
but deliver us from the evil one.

Matthew 6:9-13, NIV

WORD SEARCH

```
H  A  V  E  O  E  N  E  M  A  N
S  T  B  E  D  O  W  I  E  L  F
S  U  R  D  V  O  I  A  M  B  O
T  B  E  D  A  I  L  Y  O  U  R
A  D  A  O  O  S  L  A  C  K  G
N  E  D  N  E  V  A  E  H  M  I
D  L  F  E  D  A  E  L  A  O  V
E  H  R  D  F  L  A  I  L  D  E
B  V  O  D  A  O  R  N  L  G  N
T  E  M  P  T  A  T  I  O  N  O
O  R  I  N  H  S  H  S  W  I  T
R  U  T  H  E  G  I  V  E  K  A
S  E  R  G  R  U  Y  A  D  O  T
```

Find all the words of the Lord's Prayer in our Word
Search. If a word appears more than once in the
prayer, it is listed only one time in the Word Search.

What does it mean to be a Christian?

To find part of what it means to be a Christian first do the math problems. Write the answers in the box right below the problem. Now look at the code below to see what letter that number stands for. Write that letter in the box below the number.

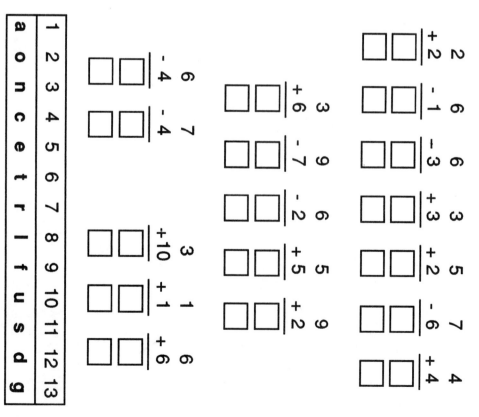

$$\begin{array}{r} 2 \\ +2 \\ \hline \end{array}$$
$$\begin{array}{r} 6 \\ -1 \\ \hline \end{array}$$
$$\begin{array}{r} 6 \\ -3 \\ \hline \end{array}$$
$$\begin{array}{r} 3 \\ +3 \\ \hline \end{array}$$
$$\begin{array}{r} 5 \\ +2 \\ \hline \end{array}$$
$$\begin{array}{r} 7 \\ -6 \\ \hline \end{array}$$
$$\begin{array}{r} 4 \\ +4 \\ \hline \end{array}$$

$$\begin{array}{r} 3 \\ +6 \\ \hline \end{array}$$
$$\begin{array}{r} 7 \\ -7 \\ \hline \end{array}$$
$$\begin{array}{r} 9 \\ -2 \\ \hline \end{array}$$
$$\begin{array}{r} 6 \\ +5 \\ \hline \end{array}$$
$$\begin{array}{r} 5 \\ +2 \\ \hline \end{array}$$
$$\begin{array}{r} 9 \\ +6 \\ \hline \end{array}$$

$$\begin{array}{r} 6 \\ -4 \\ \hline \end{array}$$
$$\begin{array}{r} 7 \\ -4 \\ \hline \end{array}$$
$$\begin{array}{r} 3 \\ +10 \\ \hline \end{array}$$
$$\begin{array}{r} 1 \\ +1 \\ \hline \end{array}$$
$$\begin{array}{r} 6 \\ +6 \\ \hline \end{array}$$

1	2	3	4	5	6	7	8	9	10	11	12	13
a	o	n	c	e	t	r	l	f	u	s	d	g

Connect the dots to find a picture of a church building.

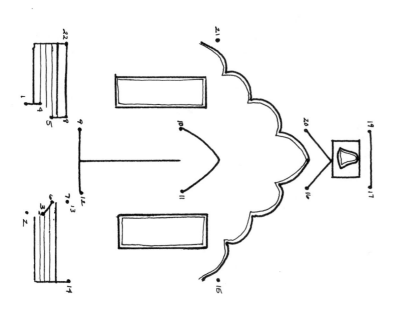

Cross out the words below as you hear them in this morning's service.

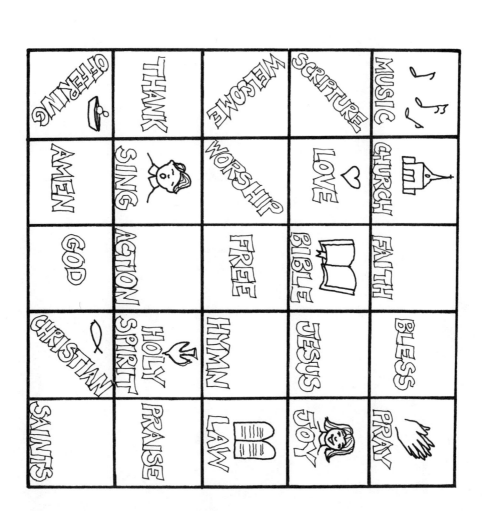

5 in a row? You're a WINNER!

ELDERS

WATCH OVER
THE LORD'S
SUPPER

WATCH OVER THE
PASTOR'S
PREACHING OF
THE WORD

WATCH OVER THE
WAY PEOPLE ARE
LIVING

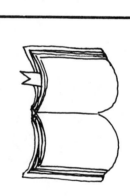

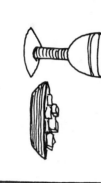

Draw a line to the correct picture.

DEACONS

TAKE OUR
OFFERINGS
EACH WEEK

BRING GIFTS
TO THE NEEDY

USE OUR
MONEY IN
GOOD WAYS

God's House

We usually treat our houses in a special way.

The church is God's house, and we want to treat it in a special way, too.

How can we make our church a good place to be for worship, learning, and friendship?

In the pictures at the right, draw in the missing parts. They are things that would help our church (God's house) be a special place.

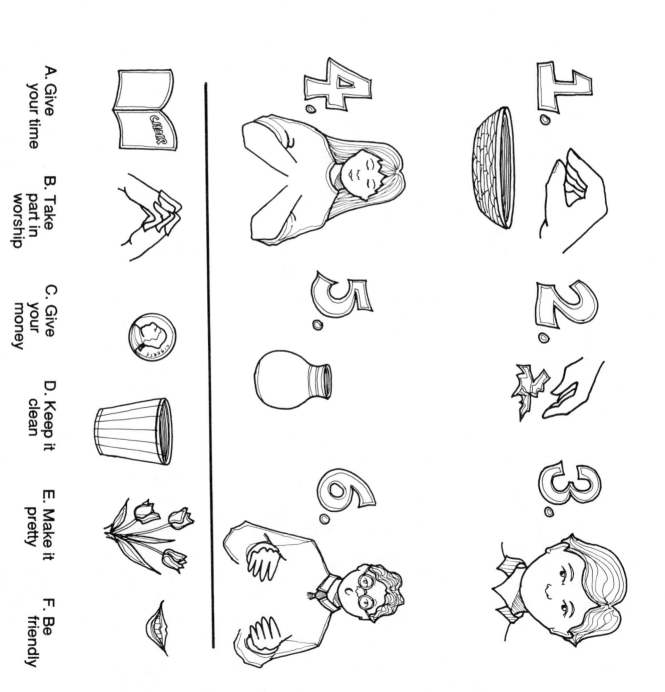

A. Give your time

B. Take part in worship

C. Give your money

D. Keep it clean

E. Make it pretty

F. Be friendly

On this page draw something you like about church.

Music is important at our church. Pay attention to our music today and do the following:

1. Print this word.

   HYMN _____

   A hymn is a song of praise to God.

2. Find each hymn we will be singing today and do your best to sing along.

3. Count the number of times the choir sings.

   _____

4. Circle the kinds of instruments that are played in church today.

   guitar   piano   bells

   organ   violin   flute

5. Does the choir do something special today? What is it?

6. Copy the words from Psalm 147:1 and 149:1 on these lines _____

How well do you know your Church Family?

Our Mystery Person last week was

_____.

_____ and

_____ were the first

to guess correctly. Congratulations, Kids!

Clues for our Mystery Person this week are:

- is the youngest of 3 boys in his family
- name is in the Bible (2 Sam. 7:2)
- last name starts with one of the last letters in the alphabet.

If you think you know, tell _____

_____.

The first 5 to get it right will get prizes this week!

You Are Special!

Jesus knows your name. You are very special to Him. What are some special things that Jesus must know about you? Use the letters in your name and write some things about yourself: what you do, what you like to eat, what you look like, etc.

Sample ideas:

Here's one about Rev. T

liv **E** s in Hudsonville

a **D** ad of 4

Preaches God's **W** ord

pr **A** ys a lot

R ides a bike

stu **D** ies a lot

Here's one about Mrs. Beute

a **M** other of 4

brown h **A** ir

loves child **R** en

bus **Y** with church school

Start at the arrow. Write down every other letter to get the name of our guest pastor. Draw a face for him.

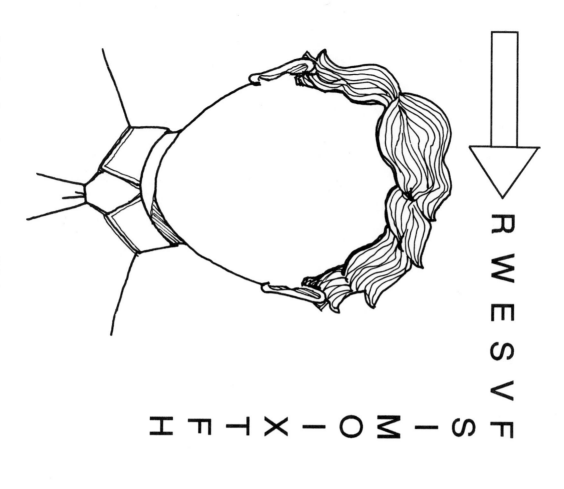

R W E S V F S I M O X T F H

In just a few days a very special day will be here.

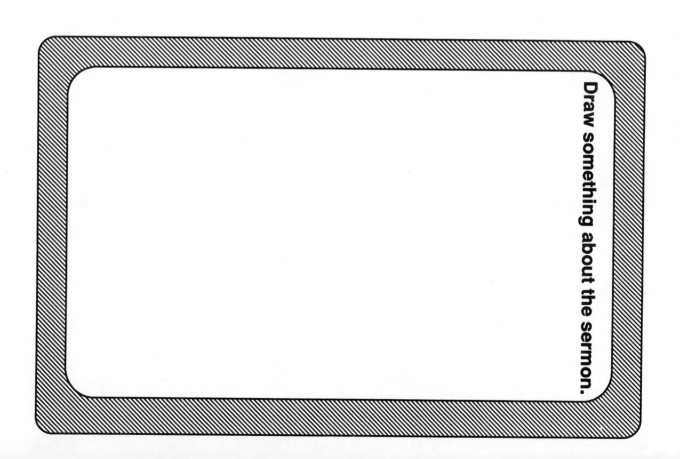

Draw something about the sermon.

See if you can find a bow, sailboat, mittens, ice cream cone, top, and a gingerbread man hidden in this picture. Then color it and decorate the cake.

A Family Experience:
Try a family hug today! It's easy to hug one person but try to get everyone together for one big hug. Watch out, there should be lots of smiles!

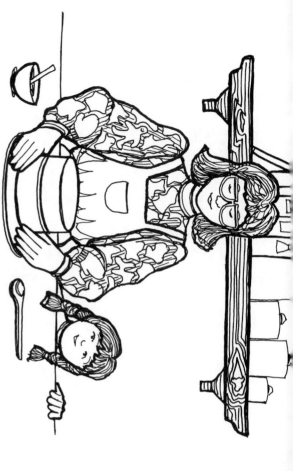

Can you find 5 musical instruments hidden in this picture?

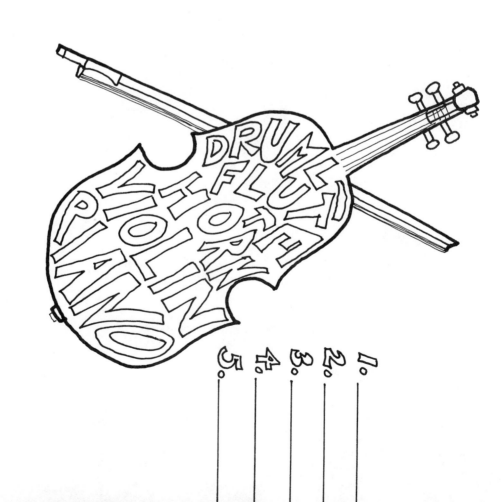

1.
2.
3.
4.
5.

Find each of the words from this Bible verse in the puzzle below. Circle them. Words may be across, down, diagonal, or backwards.

"Let us come before his presence with thanksgiving, and make a joyful noise unto him with psalms."

(Psalm 95:2)

```
A J B Z F S I H D K M P
C O T N U T B E F O R E
L Y U Z F Q G H F E Q H
W F S O S M L A S P J T
S U N M C P K E W V N I
N L H V O N N J H T I W
E K H Y M C L U T K S O
X C H M E W E T C M O E
G N I V J G S K N A H T
K V M U D A I A X K O O
N O T R N H O G T E L S
P Z J D J O N Y R H N A
```

"Come, let us bow down and worship, let us kneel before the Lord our Maker."

Psalm 95:6

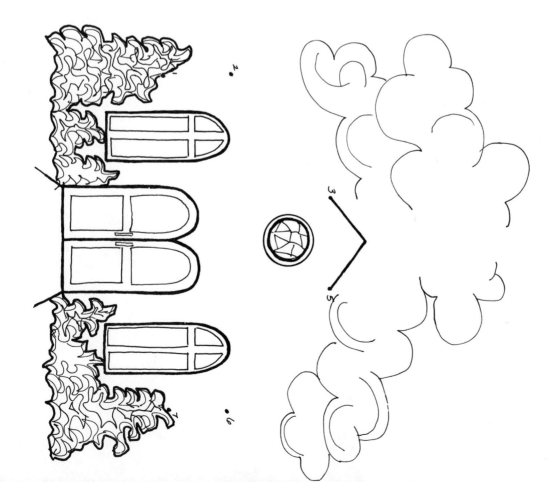

Follow the maze to see how God might call children to be of use in His Church.

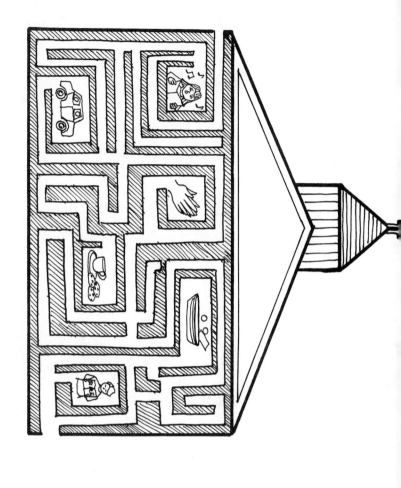

God doesn't use us just in the church. Draw a picture of how you might serve God in your everyday life. Hint: Perhaps visiting a sick friend, being kind, or bringing food to a poor family.

What do you know about the church? Start with the "J" and write every other letter for the answer.

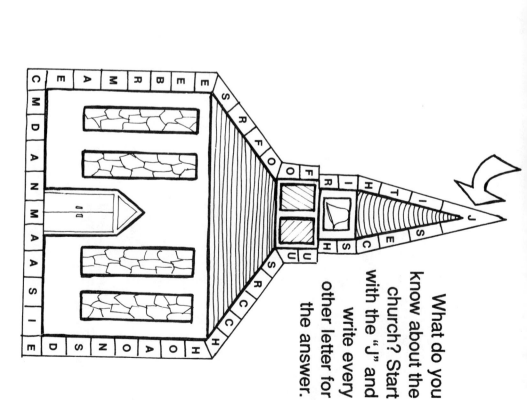

Jesus' prayer on the cross was one asking God to forgive his enemies. We can learn from Jesus' example. Which of these things should you learn to forgive for? Remember it's going to be hard at first.

Circle the letter in the YES or NO box—then put the circled letters on the lines below.

	Yes	No
When someone tattles on you.	F	A
When your friends tease you.	O	B
When someone trips you on purpose.	R	C
When your best friend saves you a seat on the bus.	D	G
When someone hits you.	I	E
When you get a birthday present.	F	V
When someone tells a lie about you.	E	G
When someone says something nice about you.	H	N
When your friend breaks your special toy.	E	I
When someone steals something of yours.	S	J
When someone pushes ahead of you in line for lunch.	S	K

_____ _____ _____ _____ shows *God's Power* in responding to evil.

As Christians Jesus called us "the salt of the earth." We are all blessed with talents to use to serve God on this earth. Some people are good singers, while others can draw well. Some are good at sports, while others do crafts well.

These talents are a:
[write the opposites]

☐☐☐ or bad

☐☐☐ or out

☐☐☐ or thin

___ ___ or cold

You are the salt of the earth, too. Circle the talents you have been given. How could you use these to serve God, the giver?

___ ___ or on

___ ___ or girls

☐☐☐ or take

___ ___ or yes

___ ___ or up

visiting   build things   making friends

drawing   crafts   writing   cooking   teaching

cheering up others   singing   reading to others   praying

caring for animals   sports   babysitting   playing the piano

The pastor's sermon today is about being

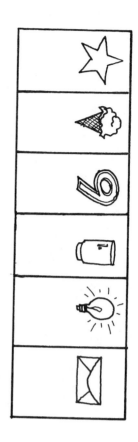

or being

(Write the beginning letter of each picture in the space below.)

He will ask which is better. Listen to the sermon and see if you can give the right answer.

Talk to someone about it at home today.

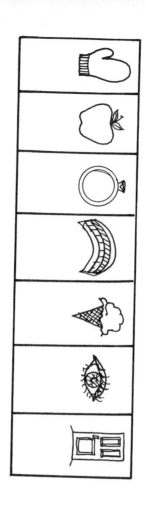

Poem People

Match the short poems to the correct people by drawing a line to connect them.

A male in a whale   David

The fall of a wall   Zacchaeus

A "he" in a tree   Joshua

A mighty sling for a future king   Jonah

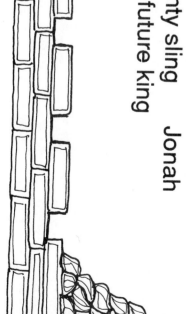

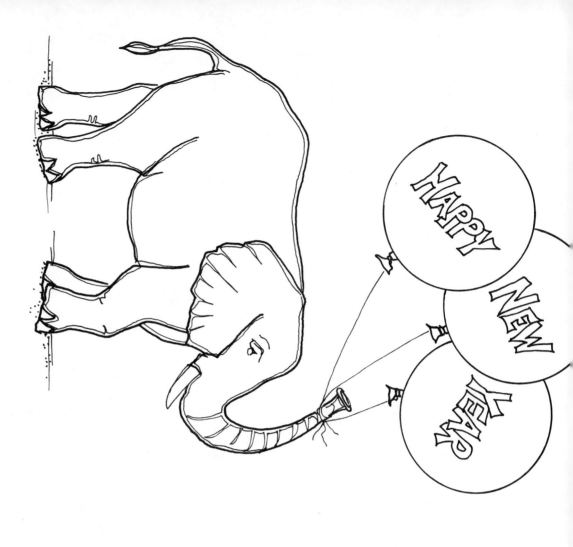

This week the ground was covered with snow! The Bible tells us that if we say we're sorry for our sins they will be forgiven and we will be as white as snow.

Today we confess our sins
A. silently
B. by singing
C. by speaking to God

After we confess our sins we hear our pastor read about God
A. forgiving
B. scolding
C. loving

(Ask an adult for the right answers.)

Ecclesiastes 3:1 tells us there is a time for everything. Look up this passage and answer the following questions.

1. How many things does it say in verses 2–8 that there is time for?

_____

2. Can you think of some other things that there is time for?

3. Read verse 12. What is the best thing for us?

4. How can we be happy?

5. Draw a picture of some good things you can do.

Solve the puzzle for the message.

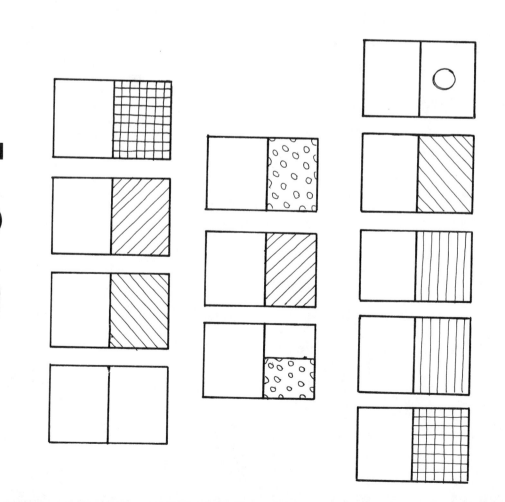

1 9 8

W E R A P Y N H

MOTHER'S DAY

I LOVE YOU BECAUSE:

Make a card or picture for dad.
Fill it with love and don't forget to sign it!

Read Acts 2. Do you recognize any Pentecost symbols in our picture?

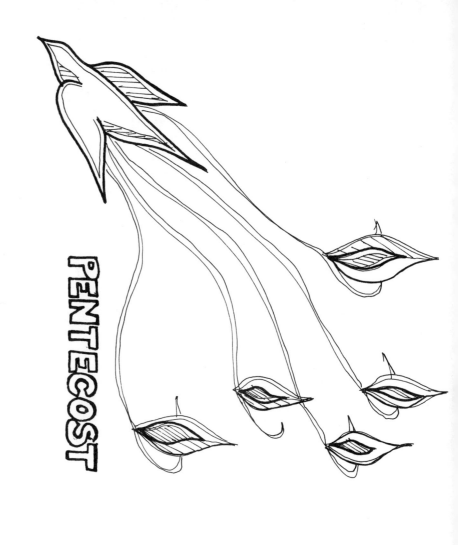

PENTECOST

PENTECOST SUNDAY

THE BIRTHDAY OF THE CHURCH

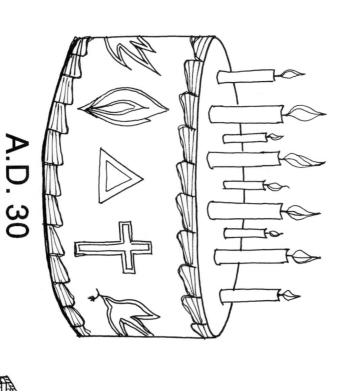

How old is the Church today?

A.D. 30

$$1988 - 30 = \underline{\hspace{2cm}}$$

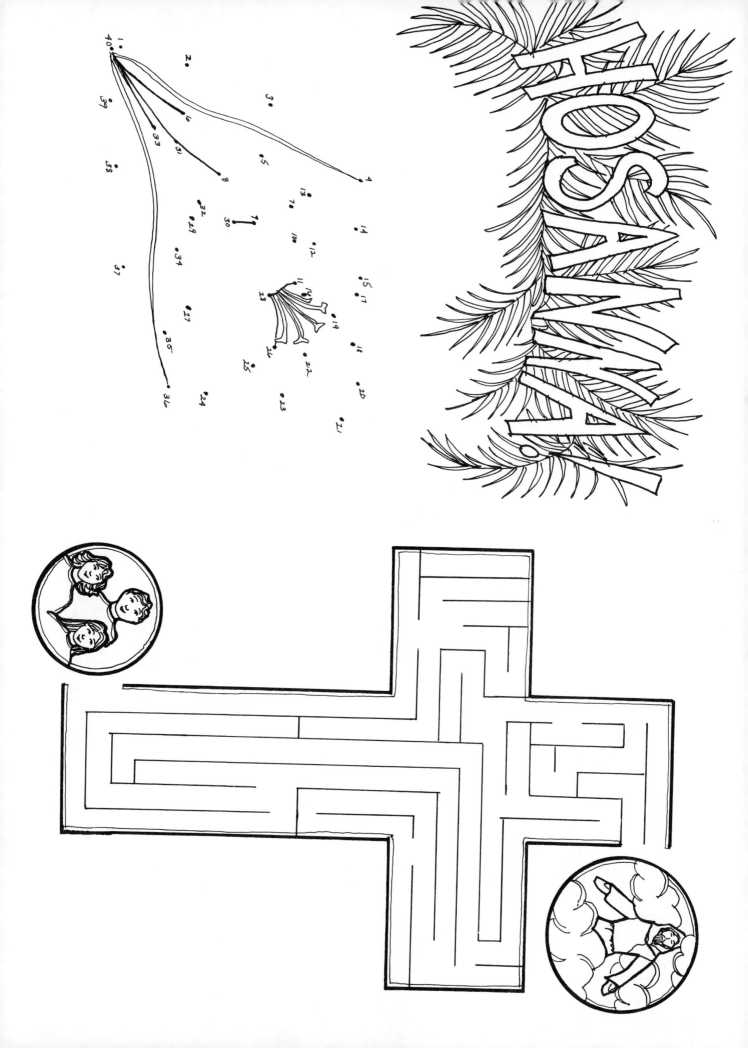

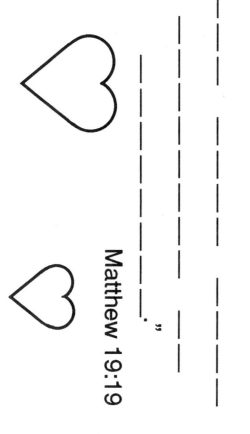

HIDDEN MESSAGE

Color in the squares that have an "X" in the corner. Put the remaining letters on the lines below to find a command that we should practice every day.

N	A	O	T	N	H	D	E	L	D	O	T
S	O	C	V	O	E	L	Y	O	O	U	R
I	N	N	T	H	E	I	E	G	X	E	S
F	H	B	O	R	A	O	S	R	Y	A	U
M	E	S	S	R	S	E	A	L	F	G	E	Q

" _ _ _ _ _   _ _ _ _ _ _ _ _ _

_ _ _ _   _ _ _ _ _ _ _ . "

Matthew 19:19

Look at the words in the signs. Write the word that:

1. begins with D and ends with o. _ _ _ _

2. begins with N and ends with t. _ _ _ _

3. begins with T and ends with e. _ _ _ _

4. begins with W and ends with t. _ _ _ _

5. begins with B and ends with s. _ _ _ _

6. begins with T and ends with o. _ _ _ _

7. begins with O and ends with s. _ _ _ _

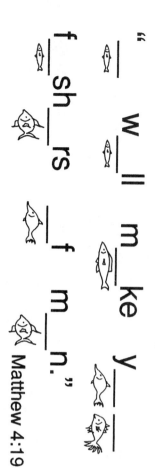

" __ w __ ll __ m __ ke __ y __

f __ sh __ rs __ __ f __ m __ n. "

Matthew 4:19

To read our Mission Message supply the necessary vowels.

a =  e = 🐟 i = 🐟 o = 🐟 u = 🐟

Bible Resolutions

Match these resolutions with the Bible people who made them.

But as for me and my household, we will serve the Lord.

For I resolved to know nothing while I was with you except Jesus Christ and him crucified.

Look, Lord! Here and now I give half of my possessions to the poor, and if I have cheated anybody out of anything, I will pay back four times the amount.

For we cannot help speaking about what we have seen and heard.

So will I go in unto the king, which is not according to the law; and if I perish, I perish.

Even if I have to die with you, I will never disown you.

I issue a decree that in every part of my kingdom people must fear and reverence the God of Daniel. For he is the living God and he endures forever.

Don't urge me to leave you or to turn back from you. Where you go I will go, and where you stay I will stay. Your people will be my people and your God my God.

Ruth (1:16)

Zacchaeus (Luke 19:8)

Esther (4:16)

King Darius (Dan. 6:26)

Peter and John (Acts 4:20)

Peter (Matt. 26:35)

Paul (1 Cor. 2:2)

Joshua (24:15)

WORD MAZE

Trace the path of the memory verse through the maze of letters. What shape do you see?

"THY WORD HAVE I HID IN MINE HEART, THAT I MIGHT NOT SIN AGAINST THEE."

Psalm 119:11

```
T H A Z H E L L O E E H T T Q
O Y H W A T E R M O O R G S U
E W A D I S C I P L E S G N O
O B B O E A R M T H A R N O I
R U S S H O P T U R T A I W A
J D A Q E W I N E O I J D G S
E H U U N O W O R D M O D A U
S A L A Y I F B R I D E E N G
U V Q Y R A M K G J V W X I A
S E I H I D I N H T N O T S R
```

Find the missing letter in each line to solve the message listed vertically at the right.

ABCDEFHIJKLMNOPQRSTUVWXYZ ____

ABCDEFGHIJKLMNOPQRSTUVWXYZ ____

ABCDEFGHIJKLMNPQRSTUVWXYZ ____

ABCDEFGHIJKLMNPQSTUVWXYZ ____

ABCDEFGHIJKLMNOPQSTUVWXYZ ____

ABCDEFGHIJKLMNOPQRSTUVWXZ ____

ABCDEFGHIJKLMNOPQRSTUVWXYZ ____

ABCDEFGHIJKLMNOPQRSTUVWXYZ ____

ABCDEFGHIJKLMNPQRSTUVWXYZ ____

ABCDEFGHIJKLMNPQRSTUVWXYZ ____

ABCDEFHIJKLMNOPQRSTUVWXYZ ____

ABCEFGHIJKLMNOPQRSTUVWXYZ ____

ABCDEFGHIJKLMNOPQRSTUVWXYZ ____

ABCDEFGHIJKLMNOPQRSTUVWXYZ ____

ABCDEFGHIJKLMOPQRSTUVWXYZ ____

ABCDEFGHIJKLMNOPQRSUVWXYZ ____

ABDFGHIJKLMNOPQRSTUVWXYZ ____

ABCDEFGIJKLMNOPQRSTUVWXYZ ____

ABCDEFGHIJKLMNOPQRSTUVWXYZ ____

ABCDEFGHJKLMNOPQRSTUVWXYZ ____

ABCDEFGHIJKLMNOPQRSTUVWXYZ ____

ABCDEFGHIJKLMNOPQRSTUVWXYZ ____

ABCDEFHIJKLMNOPQRSTUVWXYZ ____

ABCDEFGHIJKLMNOPQRSTUVWXYZ ____

ABCDFGHIJKLMNOPQRSTUVWXYZ ____

ABCDEFGHIJKLMNOPQRSTUVWXYZ ____

ABCDEFGHIJKLMNOPQRSTUVWXYZ ____

ABCDFGHIJKLMNOPQRSTUVWXYZ ____

ABCDEFGHIJKLMNOPQRTUVWXYZ ____

ABCDEFGHIJKLMNOPQRSUVWXYZ ____

Draw a line to the biblical occupation of each person listed below.

ARMY CAPTAIN	AARON
CARPENTER	ALEXANDER
CENTURION	AMOS
COPPERSMITH	AQUILA
CUP BEARER	CORNELIUS
EVANGELIST	DANIEL
FISHERMAN	DAVID
HERDSMAN	ESTHER
HUNTER	EZRA
KING	JOSEPH
MISSIONARY	LUKE
PHYSICIAN	LYDIA
PRIEST	MALCHUS
PROPHET	MATTHEW
QUEEN	NAAMAN
SCRIBE	NEHEMIAH
SELLER OF PURPLE	NIMROD
SERVANT	ONESIMUS
SHEPHERD	PAUL
SLAVE	PETER
TAX COLLECTOR	PHILIP
TENTMAKER	SOLOMON

BIBLICAL OCCUPATION WORD FIND
(Use names and occupations listed on the left)

```
Q N E H E M A L C H U S T S U L D T C Y
U A O A M O S Y O S L A V E U O S E U R
E M D I P R E D N A X E L A R R E H P A
E R R M R S U I C C A P P M V D R P B N
N E E I U Q A O P R A I N A D V O E O
R H H H E I T L P U M N L V D M A R A I
E S P E S L L N P H Y S I C I A N P R S
A F H E C N O D R C A R P E N T E R R I
K I E N T E V F E S C E H A V T T R E S
M E S T O R J O S E P H L U A H G I E M
T Z O R E O A R M S T H U N T E R N B A
N R A L A C L E I N A D K S E W A K I N
E A L I U Q A U T S I L E G N A V E R K
T E N A A M A N A H A N A M S D R E H C S
S R E T E P S U M I S E N O M O L O S O
```

Crack the code to discover the two rules Jesus said were the most important to follow.

1

2

B D E G H I L N O R U V Y

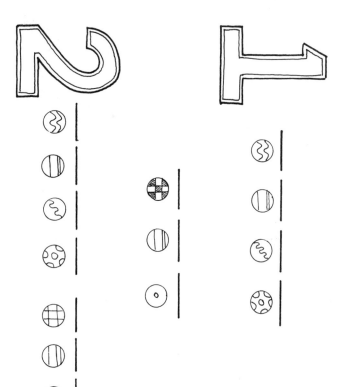

JESUS SAID:

John 15:5

YOU ARE THE

Color the letters that have an X on them.

Use the code to write the correct letter on each line.

R   B   A   N   C   E   S

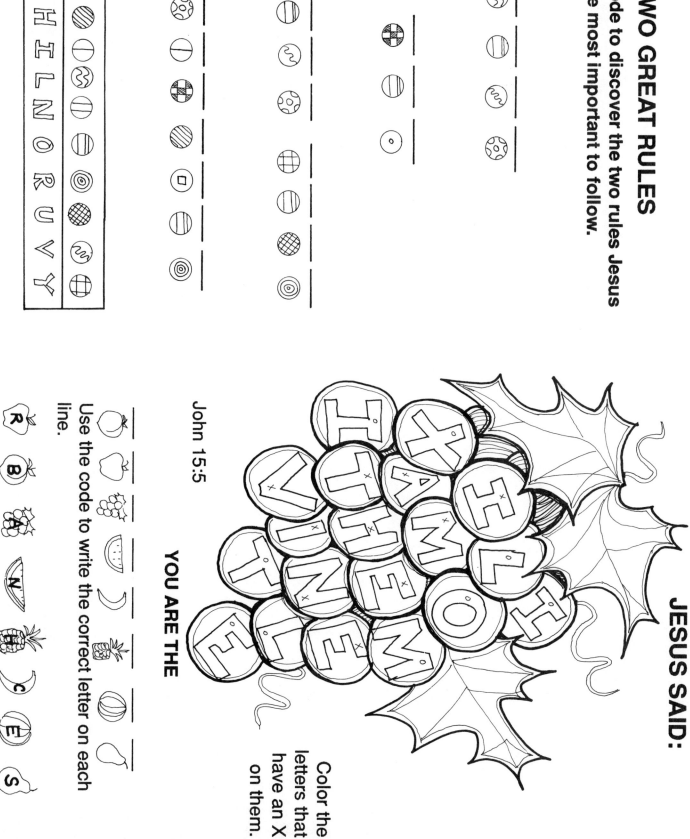

A Loving Father

The prodigal son said something that made his father very happy. What was it? Color in each of the spaces with the word "Son" in it, and you will see.

In the story of the prodigal son, the father loved both of his sons. Each of them was very special to him. Who is the father in this story like? Color in each of the spaces with the word "Father" in it, and you will see.

When we tell God that we are wrong and want to change, what does God do? Color in each space with the word "God" in it, and you will see.

CHILDREN'S BULLETIN

Go around the circle skipping every other letter. Write the letters below.

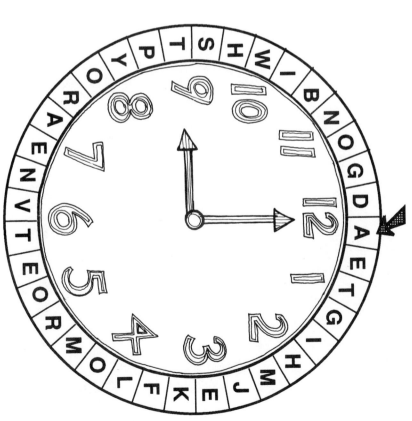

___ ___ ___ ___

___ ___ ___

Write the alphabet letter that comes before each letter already in the box.

God is the of

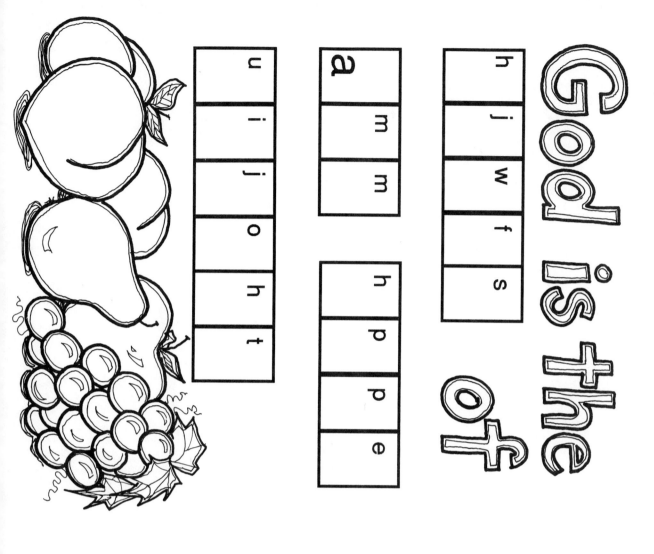

h	j	w	f	s

a	m	m

	h	p	p	e

u	i	j	o	h	t

Color the squares that have triangles. Put the
remaining letters on the lines below.

Color Squares

B○	O▷	L▷	I○	E▷	S○	R▷	E▷	T○	D○
A▷	R○	N○	E▷	Z▷	T○	I▷	P▷	H○	U▷
A▷	P○	O▷	U○	R▷	E▷	Z○	I▷	M○	N▷
H○	B▷	E▷	I○	U▷	A○	T○	R▷	A▷	T○
M○	O○	Y▷	F▷	E○	O▷	L▷	D○	R▷	W○
T▷	H○	S▷	F○	Z▷	E○	T▷	T○	G▷	Y▷
S○	N▷	H○	M▷	A○	P▷	O▷	L○	O▷	N○
S○	E○	L▷	E○	A▷	A○	G▷	I▷	O○	W▷
S○	E▷	L○	E▷	A○	A▷	G○			D○

Matthew 5:8

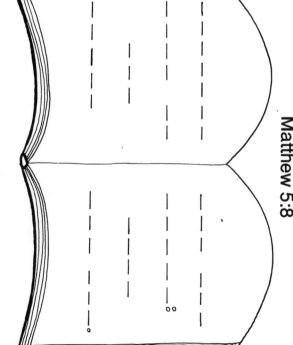

Galatians 6:7 tells us:

"A ___ ___ ___ what he ___ ___ ___."

Match the small seeds below to see what large plants you might harvest.

SMALL SEEDS

Saving empty pop cans.

Saying "hello" to a new person at school.

Studying your math hard every day.

Saying "thank you" to your mother for a good meal.

Making a sign for the church picnic.

Helping the man who lives next door when he needs it.

Sending money to a hunger fund.

LARGE PLANTS

Many people are fed and lives are saved.

A happy mother who enjoys fixing meals for her family.

Fifty people come to the picnic.

A friendship that lasts all of your life.

A church collects 500 cans a month for a recycling project.

A good report card.

A person who tells everyone that kids are great.

Sometimes our hearts are like deep dark caves. All kinds of bad feelings and habits hide there, like goblins in the night. Sometimes they get out and bother us. Read these verses to find what goblins may be hiding in you. Write names on each of the goblins.

Ephesians 4:31   Ephesians 5:4
1 John 3:15   Colossians 3:8, 9

BEWARE! GREED

Now read 1 John 1:9 and write here what God will do when you ask Him to. _____

_____

Starting with W and moving clockwise, color every other letter.

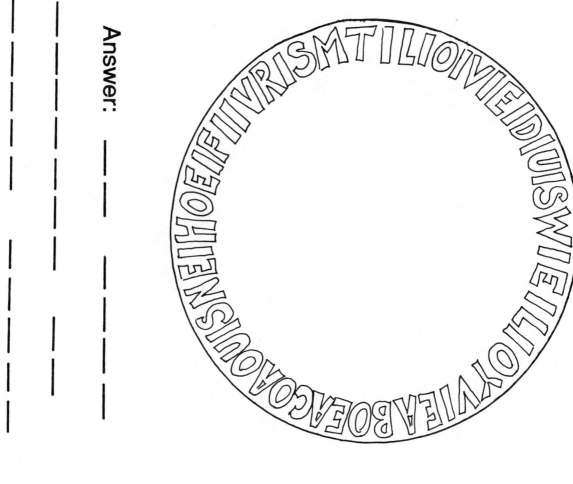

Answer: ___ ___ ___

___ ___ ___ ___

1 John 4:19

People will know that we are Christians by the way we act. Cover up the bad actions by coloring them, so we can see only the good ones.

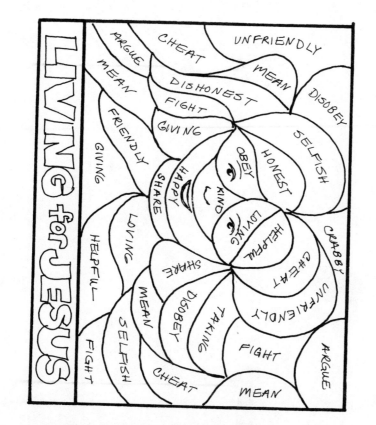

LIVING for JESUS

CHILDREN'S BULLETIN

Today Is
Church School
Award Sunday

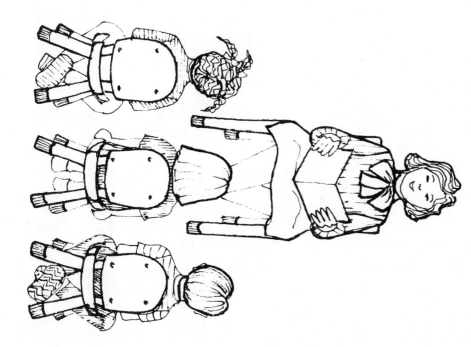

FAMILY TIME
TABLE TALK

1. Thank God for our Church School teachers.
2. Pray for moms and dads in your prayers.
3. Read I Samuel 1:3-11 and 19-20 about a very special mother.

This puzzle is about an Old Testament prophet. Put the first letter of each clue in the space to find his name.

___ To live we must _____ food.

___ God so _____ the world.

___ _____ am the light of the world.

___ The walls of _____ fell down.

___ A good red fruit is an _____.

___ It's fun to sing _____ Birthday.

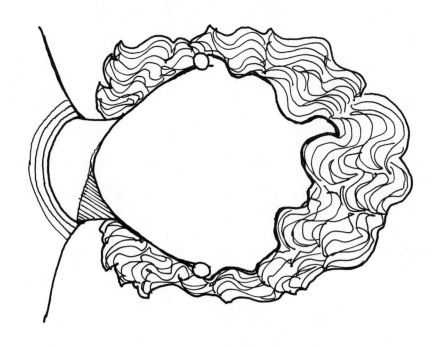

Draw your super mom.

Make a Mother's Day card for your mother.

THE TEN COMMAMANDMENTS

1. You shall have no other gods before me

2. YOU SHALL NOT MAKE FOR YOURSELF AN IDOL

3. You shall not misuse the name of the Lord your God

4. OBSERVE THE SABBATH DAY BY KEEPING IT HOLY

5. HONOR YOUR FATHER AND MOTHER

6. You shall not MURDER

7. You shall not commit adultery

8. YOU SHALL NOT STEAL

9. You shall not give false testimony against your neighbor

10. YOU SHALL NOT COVET

THE TEN COMMANDMENTS

1. You shall have no other gods before me
2. YOU SHALL NOT MAKE FOR YOURSELF AN IDOL
3. You shall not misuse the name of the Lord your God
4. OBSERVE THE SABBATH DAY BY KEEPING IT HOLY
5. HONOR YOUR FATHER AND MOTHER
6. YOU SHALL NOT MURDER
7. You shall not commit adultery
8. YOU SHALL NOT STEAL
9. You shall not give false testimony against your neighbor
10. YOU SHALL NOT COVET

Valentine's Day

God sends people to take care of us and love us. Draw a ♡ on the people we should love. When we love others we make Jesus feel ☺.

BOYS, GIRLS, MOMS, & DADS
BE SURE TO READ THIS
BEFORE COLORING THE VALENTINE!

In your bulletin is a valentine for you to finish. Decorate it with red or white ribbon, yarn, lace scraps, or whatever and be sure to color it neatly.

Write a cheerful message to a SENIOR CITIZEN. *We ask you not to write their name on the card please.* We will have addressed envelopes to put each card in, as we want to be sure each of our seniors receive one.

Be sure to write your full name. When you are finished, put your card in the special mail box at church. Be sure to have them finished by February 8. Thank you.

Using the code below, translate this message.

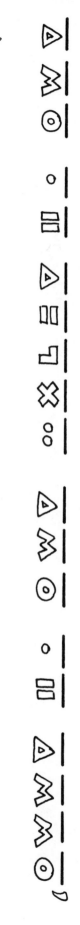

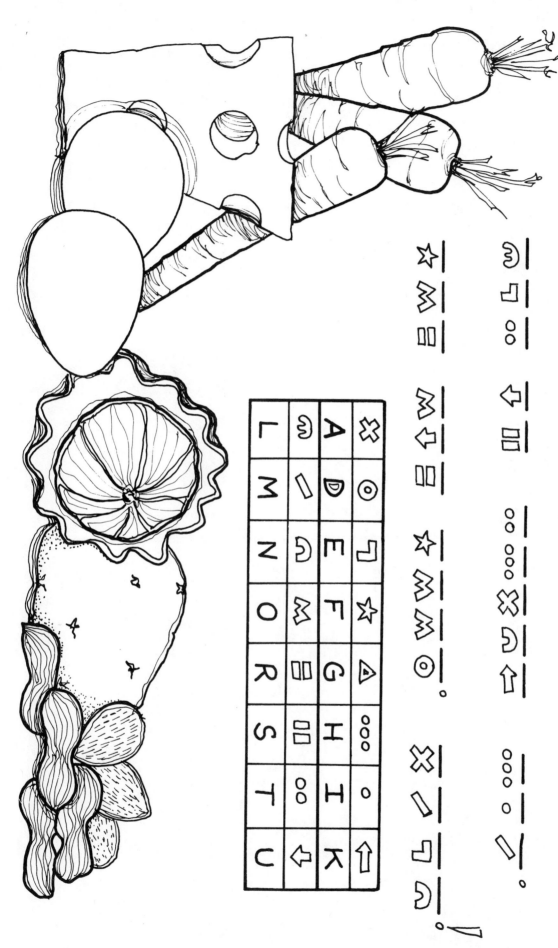

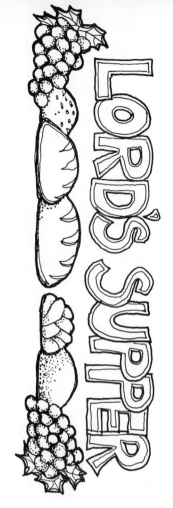

THE LORD'S SUPPER

Put the first letter of the object below the line **ON** that line.

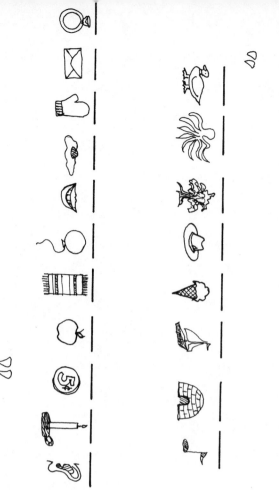

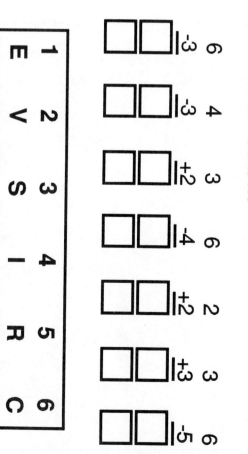

The Cross and the Towel
John 13:1-11

Jesus' life was one of giving and serving. Just before they had the Passover Feast Jesus washed each of the disciples' feet—a real servant's job. Would you like to wash people's feet who were walking on a dusty road in sandals? Jesus did it. He also expects our lives to be one of . . .

Solve the math problem then look at the code to see which letter should go in the box below.

☐☐	☐☐	☐☐	☐☐	☐☐	☐☐	☐☐
6 −3	4 −3	3 +2	6 −4	2 +2	3 +3	6 −5

1	2	3	4	5	6
E	V	S	I	R	C

Lord's Supper

This morning we celebrate the Lord's Supper. This helps remind us of Jesus' sacrifice when He died for us.

The Mystery Picture will be of something that also reminds us of His death. To finish the picture, pick the correct answer to each question. Color in the square that has the same number as your answer. (The first one is done for you.)

1. During Communion the wine is a sign of:
   A-2 running water
   B-4 Jesus' blood

2. The bread is a sign of:
   E-3 Jesus' body
   D-1 the wheat harvest

3. During Communion we remember:
   A-5 Jesus' birth
   B-3 Jesus' death

4. To take Communion we must:
   D-5 be perfect
   D-3 be sorry for our sins

5. We also remember that:
   A-3 our sins are forgiven
   C-4 Moses gave us the Law

6. When Jesus celebrated the first Lord's Supper, He was with:
   C-2 His family
   B-2 His disciples

7. Jesus' death paid for:
   B-5 His sins
   C-3 our sins

Mystery Picture

	1	2	3	4	5
A					
B					
C			■		
D					
E					

THE LAST SUPPER

$$\overline{67} \quad \overline{96} \quad \overline{15} \quad \overline{48} \quad \overline{83} \quad \overline{25} \quad \overline{15} \quad \overline{55}$$

$$\overline{6} \quad \overline{3} \quad \overline{10} \quad \overline{3} \quad \overline{10} \quad \overline{29} \quad \overline{6} \quad \overline{77} \quad \overline{55} \quad \overline{39} \quad \overline{3}$$

$$\overline{25} \quad \overline{35} \quad \overline{10} \quad \overline{3} \, .$$

O	C	E	B
15 $+10$	32 $+7$	20 -17	56 $+12$

H	M	I	S
84 $+12$	72 -62	45 -30	36 $+12$

T	N	A	R
94 -27	33 $+22$	30 $+47$	58 -52

D	F
98 -15	17 $+18$

Solve the puzzle by first doing the math problems. Then put the letter on the blanks above.

Come, for the Feast Is Spread

What sacrament are we celebrating this morning?

or _____.

Why do the bread and wine remind us of Jesus' death? When we break the bread, we remember the pain Jesus must have felt as He hung on the cross. When we pour the wine we remember the blood that came from His wounds. When we eat the bread and drink the wine, we feel close to Jesus as we remember how He gave His life so we may live.

Some words you will hear during communion this morning are: blood, body, bread, broken, cup, drink, eat, Jesus, shed, wine. Find these words below.

```
A Y I B Q H B O D Y
J J N B V G U E O H
Z E T H X P F T O W
R S S G D E A V L U
P U C B R E A D B I
C S A O C N R F T D
F R W J K I D G J Z
I X D Q N W P E O A
J N E K O R B N H B
S E K Y M L C L M S
```

Draw a picture today of the communion table up front.

Find a nine letter word telling about the Lord's Supper (hidden in this picture).

The Greek word *koinonia*, (pronounced coin-a-noya), means communion, or fellowship.

THE LORD'S SUPPER

JESUS DIED ON
THE CROSS TO
SAVE US FROM
ALL OF OUR
SINS. HE GAVE
US SOMETHING
TO ALWAYS RE-
MIND US OF THAT
FACT, TOO.

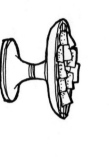

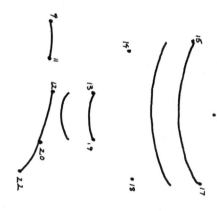

Take time to thank him today during communion.

When
Jesus
first gave
the wine
and bread
to His disciples,
He said it was
to *remind* them
of His gift of Himself
for man's salvation.

If you
color in
all of the
dotted
spaces in the
heart, you will
see something
else which will
remind you of his
great gift to us.

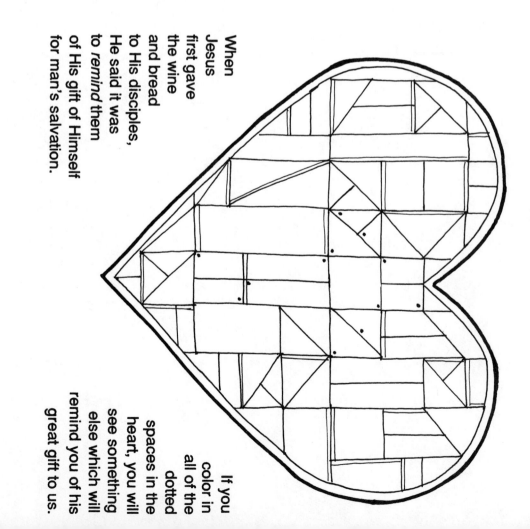

This evening we will be studying the phrase "Hallowed be thy Name" from the Lord's Prayer. How can we put into practice hallowing God's name?

Rewrite the mixed-up words. Say the sentences.

1. (seU) ☐☐ His name with all things that are (ruet) ☐☐☐.

2. (allC) ☐☐☐ to Him in every time of (eedn) ☐☐☐.

3. (ingS) ☐☐☐ to Him about His (ovel) ☐☐☐ and kindness to us.

4. (hankT) ☐☐☐ Him for everything we (aveh) ☐☐☐.

Tonight we will have Communion and the pastor will be preaching about **"Lead Us Not into Temptation."** We learn how God will always be with us. Color in all of the spaces with **Tempt** in them to see how we can feel God close when we are tempted.

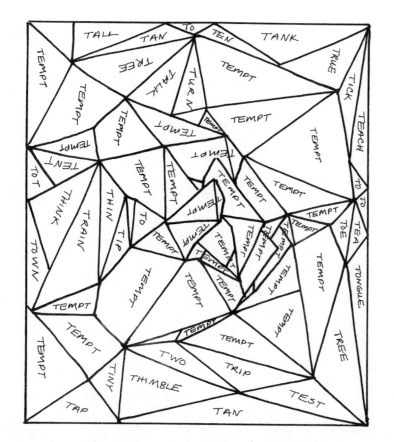

Today is another lesson in the life of Joseph. It is about

Use the code to find the answer.

____ ____ ____ ____ ____ ____ .

C	E	T
R	I	J
N	E	O

R □ ⊏ ⊓ ⌐ □ ⌐

Read the verses in Luke 12 and write this tiny creature's name here.

____ ____ ____ ____ ____

GROWING in God's family

Look up 2 Peter 3:18 on page ____ in your Bible and fill in the blanks.

"B ☐ t gr △ w ____ n th ____ –

gr __ c ____ nd
+ △ – – + △
kn ____ wl __ dg ____ f
☐ △ △
__ r L rd __ nd
+ ○ △ △ – ☐ +
S __ v __ r J s s
__ + ○ △ – +

Chr ____ st."
△

+	...	a
e	i	o
o	△	u
☐	u	

If you hear the pastor say this verse this morning put a smile on this face.

Our growing minds and Spirits

Many things help us to grow. Find these words in the puzzle below.

Growing   Preachers
Catechism   Church
Sunday School   Prayer
Parents   Calvinette
Cadet   School
Teachers   Sermon
Bible

```
A C P P D G D H L J N Z T
P A R E N T S Q V R A I S
R Q A C A L V I N E T T E
E H Y N F Y M B I L S G N
A T E A C H E R S B E N C
C X R G L A K A R J I H
H C A D E T N C I B U W J
E C A T E C H I S M P O R
R L W S C H O O L D E R C
S E R M O N S T V O O G H
I L O O H C S Y A D N U S
```

BAPTISM

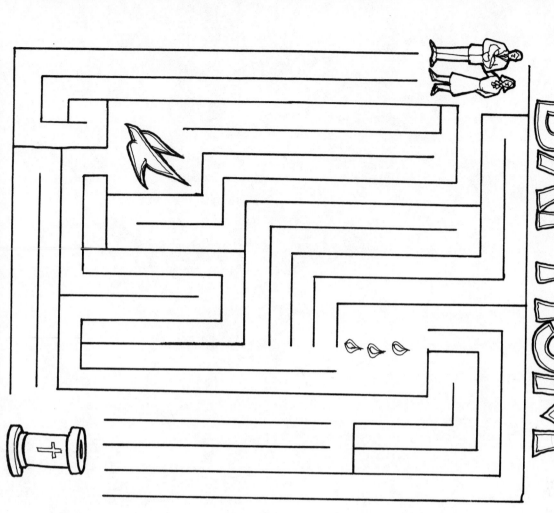

Help the parents through the maze to get their baby to the baptismal font. Note the symbols of baptism as you go through the maze.

1. _____

2. _____

What Does Baptism Mean?

1. Jesus has <u>saved</u> us from our sins.
2. Our <u>sins</u> are <u>washed</u> away.
3. God gives us a <u>new life</u>.
4. God <u>adopts</u> us as His <u>children</u>.
5. We are <u>alive</u> in <u>Christ</u>.
6. God gives us <u>power</u> to start living in loving ways.
7. He wants us to move out into the <u>world</u> as His people, doing <u>good</u> and <u>spreading</u> His (Word.)

Look for the underlined words in the puzzle. Circle them when you find them.

```
S P R E A D I N G Q
C A C G I J D P P R
H D V H W D R O W T
I O D E H S A W O V
L P N F D K M E R G
D T D I S L N R L X
R S A L I V E O D W
E A E G N I V O L U
N B F T S I R H C S
```

Complete the maze by starting at the dot and finishing at the square.

How many books of the Bible can you name that rhyme with these words?

1. Truth _____
2. Spaniel _____
3. Brings _____
4. Neater _____
5. Jester _____
6. Famous _____
7. Calms _____

Bible Families

How well do you know parents and children in the Bible? On the left are listed Biblical fathers and mothers. On the right are listed one child of each parent. Draw a line from the parent to the child.

1. Eve   Absalom
2. Noah   Samuel
3. David   Cain
4. Saul   Isaac
5. Abraham   David
6. Rebekah   Ham
7. Hannah   Jonathan
8. Jesse   Jacob

Hooray for
Dad, of course) on the birth of a baby (brother)
(and Mom and
(sister)!

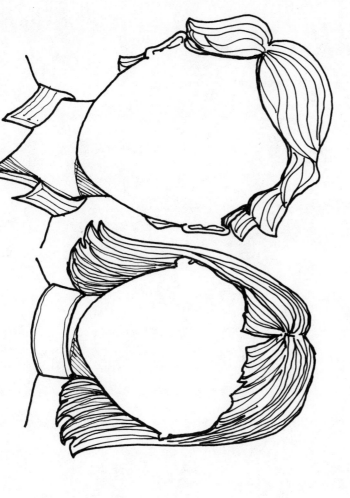

_____
(name)

DRAW A PICTURE
OF YOUR FAMILY.

PALM SUNDAY

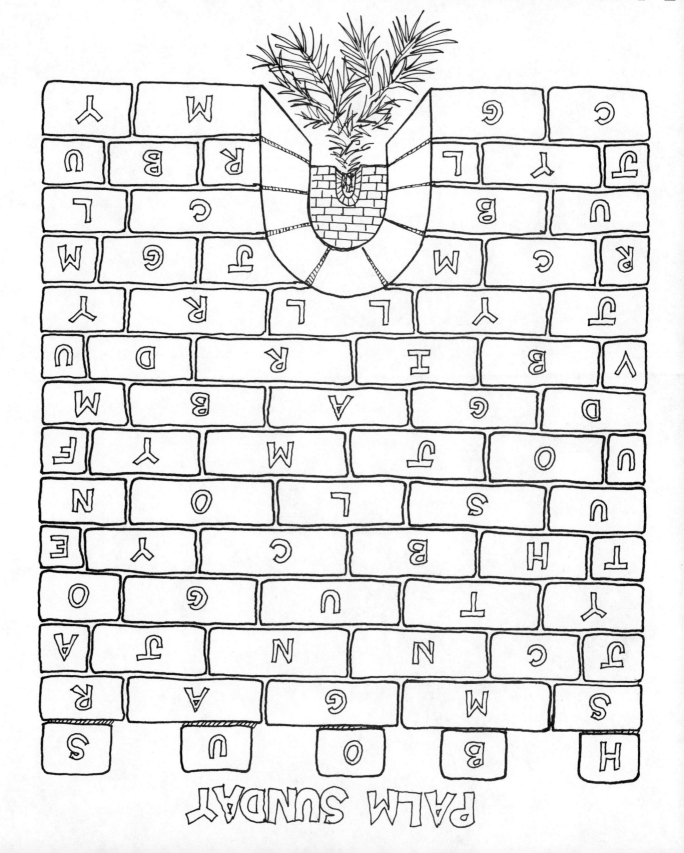

To find the message hidden on the gateway to Jerusalem, cross off all the letters that appear 5 or more times.

Where is this text found in the Bible?

_____ __ __ __ __ __ __ __

Kids, are you starting to get bored with summer? Before we all go back to school, let's go on a "Bible Picnic."

For lunch, instead of taking hot dogs or hamburgs, we'll be taking food that's mentioned in the Bible. So, take your Bible and look up the verses, then fill in the blanks.

Let's start with sandwiches. For these you'll need _____ (Eccl. 11:1) and _____ (Ps. 55:21). Fill them with _____ (1 Sam. 17:18) or lots of _____ (Ps. 105:23) or _____ (Lev. 23:12) or tuna _____ (John 21:6). You might want to bring some _____ (Job 6:6) and _____ (Matt. 13:31) to spice them up a little. Some people like just _____ (Matt. 3:4) on their _____ (Eccl. 11:1). A hard boiled _____ (Luke 11:12) with _____ (Job 6:6) always tastes good, and what is a picnic

without stuffed _____ (Mic. 6:15)? There is plenty of _____ (Hos. 9:16): _____ (Prov. 25:11), clusters of _____ (Gen. 40:10), _____ (Nah. 3:12), juicy _____ (Num. 11:5), and lots of _____ (Hos. 3:1). No ice cream, but some crunchy, salty _____ (Gen. 43:11) for dessert. For drinks, you can have _____ and _____ (Heb. 5:13) and cold _____ (Matt. 10:42). Boy, what a large _____ (Gen. 40:17) you will need in which to pack all of this! Don't forget to take _____s (Judg. 6:38), and the _____ (Josh. 5:2), and we'll need some _____s (Exod. 28:36) and _____ (Isa. 30:24). Let's hope no _____s (Prov. 6:6) join you and that it doesn't _____ (Zech. 10:1)!

HIDDEN FISH

Jesus had twelve disciples. He said, "Follow me, and I will make you fishers of men." (Matt. 4:19)

Find the twelve good fish in the stained glass window.

New Testament believers used the fish as the symbol of a Christian.

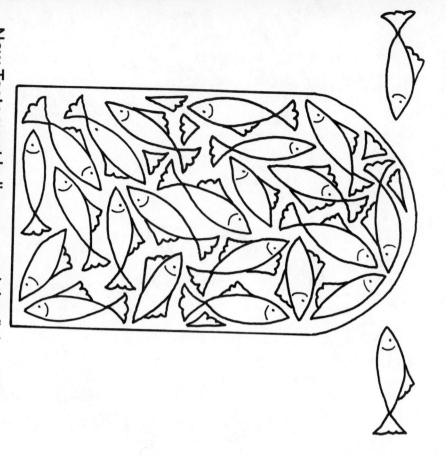

HIDDEN DOVES

The dove is a symbol which represents the Holy Spirit.

When Jesus was baptized, the Spirit descended on him like a dove. (Mark 1:10)

Find the 7 doves that are shaped just like the one at the top of the page. Add an eye to these 7 doves. Leave the doves white and color the remaining shapes different colors.

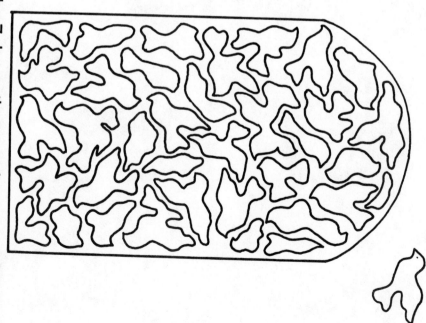

Use the first letter of each object to
write the *Good News* message below.

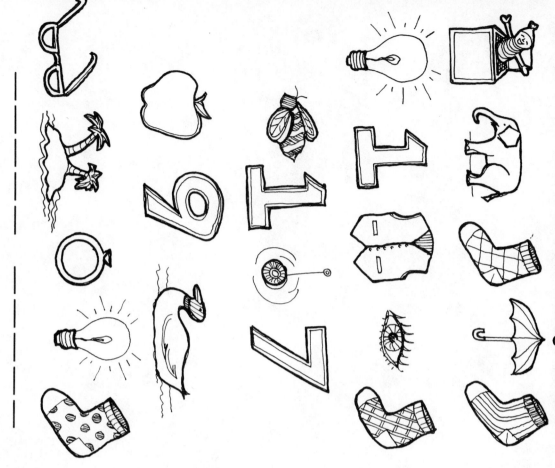

_ _ _ _ _ _ _ _   _ _ _ _ _ _ _ _

St. Patrick appeared before the pagan King of
Ireland to speak to him about the Trinity. The king
could not understand how three persons could be
in one. St. Patrick plucked a shamrock that was
growing nearby. He showed it to the king, asking
him if it were one leaf or three. The King was
unable to answer the question. Then St. Patrick
assured him that if he could not explain the mystery of the shamrock, that there was no hope of
him understanding so deep a mystery as the Holy
Trinity. The shamrock has become a well-known
symbol of the Trinity. On each leaf fill in a name of
one of the three persons of the Trinity.

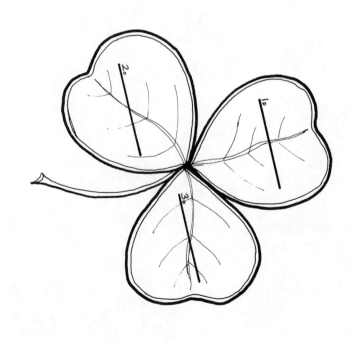

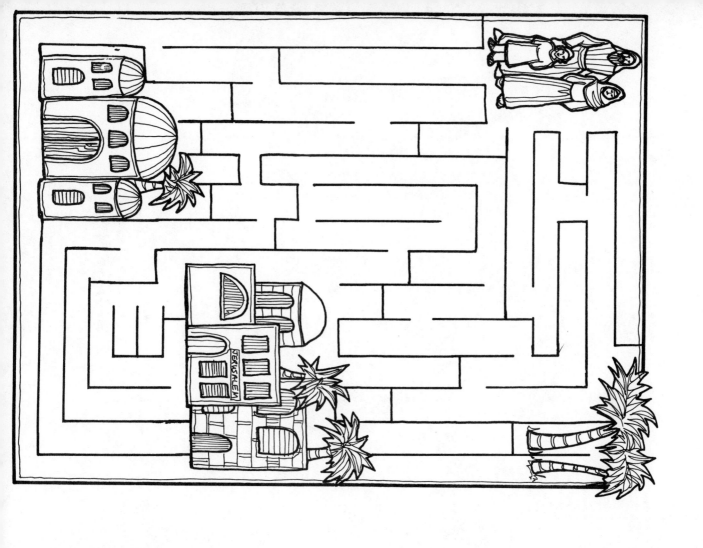

A New Year—
see it in with God!

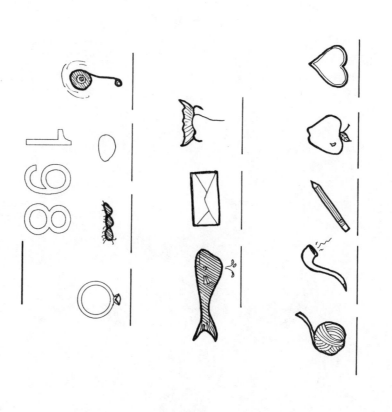

Put the first letter of the object below the line ON
that line.

Can you fill in the last blank without a clue?
Get used to it—it's here for a long time!!

Find your way through the maze to make a special message. Write each letter below as you come to it.

START

FINISH

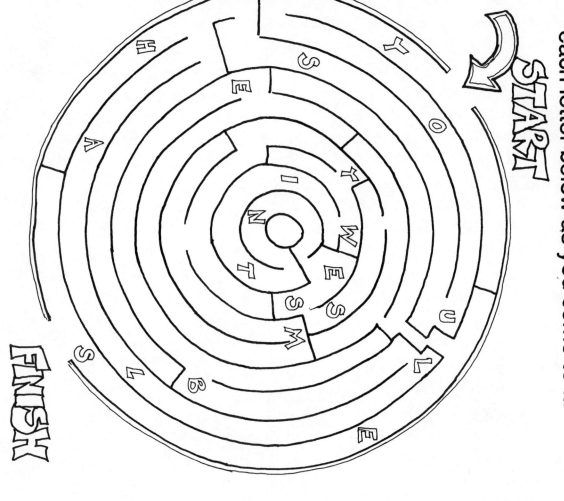

_ _ _ _

_ _ _ _ _ _ _

God gives many things to us. Find 10 things that you've been given. List three things that you can give to God.

1.

2.

3.

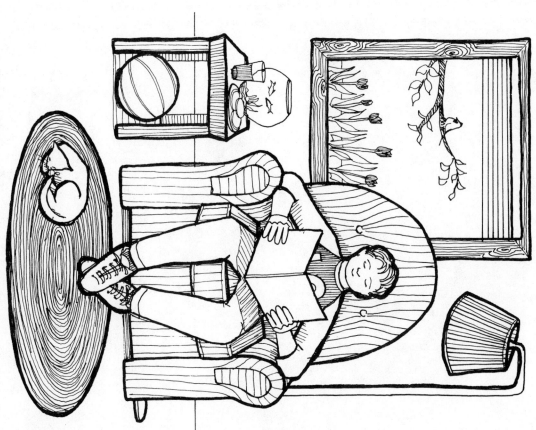

1= black
2= red
3= green
4= gray
5= pink
6= blue
7= white

1= red
2= black
3= green
4= yellow
5= blue
6= brown

1= black
2= brown
3= red
4= green
5= yellow
6= blue
7= white

1= pink
2= green
3= brown
4= yellow
5= orange
6= white
7= black
8= blue

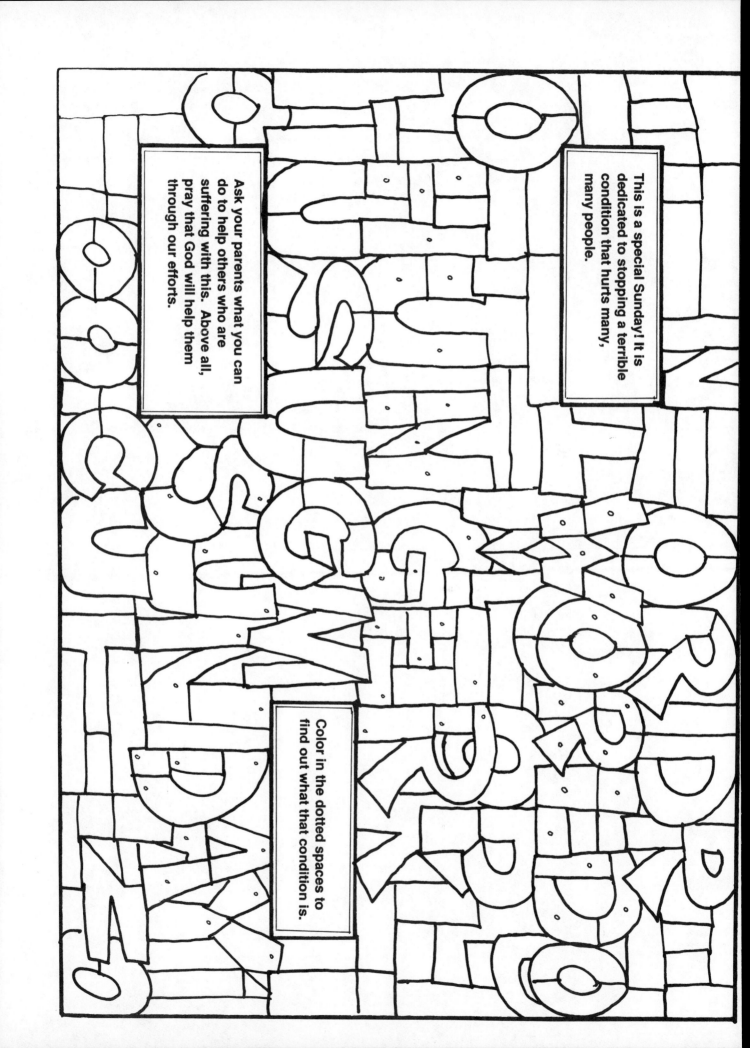

This is a special Sunday! It is dedicated to stopping a terrible condition that hurts many, many people.

Ask your parents what you can do to help others who are suffering with this. Above all, pray that God will help them through our efforts.

Color in the dotted spaces to find out what that condition is.

Read the verses Martin Luther found in the Bible by decoding this puzzle.

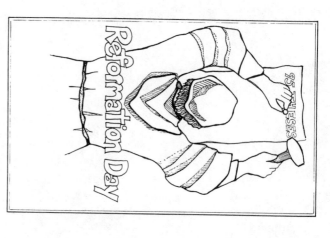

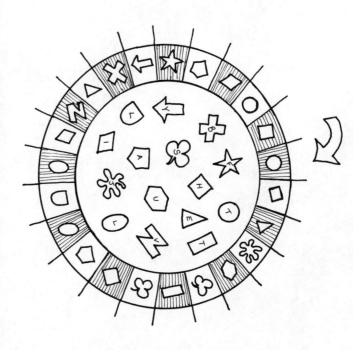

Unscramble these books of the Bible to see what books this text are found in . . .

KUABKAHK _____

ASOMRN _____

TSALAAGNI _____

Ma___tin Luther struggled ___very day trying to ___ind peace for his s___ul. While studying the Bible, he ___ead, "The just shall live by faith." Suddenly free from the chains of works, ___artin began to pre___ch the ___ruths ___n God's Word. On ___ctober 31, 1517 he ___ailed 95 thesis to the door of his church.

Use the letters of our special day to fill in the blanks. Put R in the first blank, and so on.

REFORMATION DAY

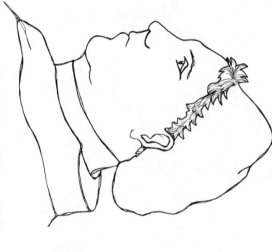

Read the story and finish filling in the blanks with the missing words.

O _____ 31 is a day for Christians to celebrate. October 31 is R _____

D _____.

A long time ago a man named M _____

L _____ nailed a paper to the door of a church. The paper started lots of trouble. It told about things that the c _____ was doing wrong. Martin Luther had been reading his

B _____ and he found out that the church was not o _____ God in many ways.

What had Martin Luther found in the Bible? The Bible says that people have s _____ in their hearts. They can't do anything to save themselves. But the church was teaching something different. The church said people could get to h _____ by paying m _____ or doing certain things.

God showed Martin Luther many things. The Bible says that salvation is a free g _____ from God. People need faith in Jesus. The Bible tells the truth about salvation through faith in Jesus. The Bible tells people the truth about how to live for the Lord in every part of life.

MISSING WORDS

heaven	sin	Bible
money	gift	Martin Luther
obeying	church	Reformation Day

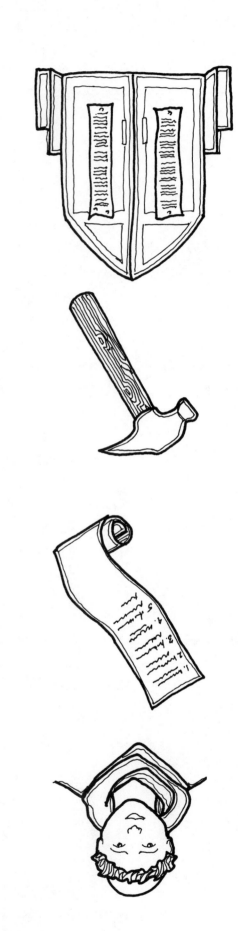

Draw a line to the matching picture.

"I SAID MY PRAYERS BEFORE YOU GOT HERE BECAUSE GOD AN' I HAD SOME SECRET THINGS TO TALK ABOUT."

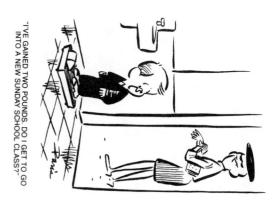

"I'VE GAINED TWO POUNDS. DO I GET TO GO INTO A NEW SUNDAY SCHOOL CLASS?"

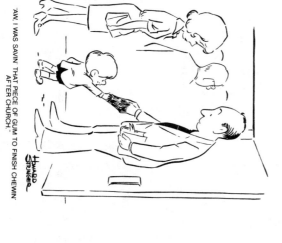

"AW, I WAS SAVIN' THAT PIECE OF GUM TO FINISH CHEWIN' AFTER CHURCH."

"NOW I KNOW HOW JOSEPH'S BROTHERS FELT WHEN HE GOT ALL TH' ATTENTION."

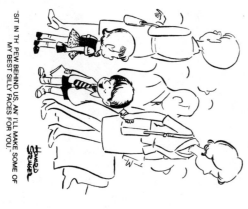

"SIT IN TH' PEW BEHIND US, AN' I'LL MAKE SOME OF MY BEST SILLY FACES FOR YOU."

"I THINK GOD MAY HAVE A PROBLEM. I'VE BEEN PRAYIN' THAT IT SNOWS SO HARD THEY HAVE TO CLOSE SCHOOL. MY MOM IS PRAYIN' THAT IT DON'T."

IT WAS WORTH A TRY.

I "DIDN'T START A FIGHT WITH TOMMY IN CHURCH! WE JUST FINISHED ONE WE STARTED YESTERDAY."

"NOTHING EXCITING EVER HAPPENS ON THIS JOB."

CHURCH NURSERY

MRS. CRAWFORD SAYS YOU USED TO CRY WHEN YOU GOT LEFT IN THE NURSERY TOO.

HOW MUCH LONGER DO I HAVE TO SIT PERFECTLY STILL?

I KNOW WHAT'S IN THE BIBLE...MY GRANDMOTHER'S SECRET RECIPE FOR GERMAN CHOCOLATE CAKE.

HOLD YOUR EARS FOR A MINUTE. I WANT TO TELL GOD A SECRET.

GOD THINKS I SHOULD SLEEP IN HERE 'TIL HE'S FINISHED MAKIN' IT THUNDER AN' LIGHTNIN'.

WE'RE TRYIN' FOR PERFECT ATTENDANCE IN OUR SUNDAY SCHOOL...IF YOU MISS NEXT SUNDAY, I'LL PUNCH YOU IN TH' NOSE.

COULD WE HAVE A MOMENT OF PRAYER TOGETHER BEFORE YOU LOOK AT MY REPORT CARD?

DADDY DIDN'T HAVE TO STAND IN TH' CORNER WHEN HE SAID THAT WORD.

"OF COURSE NOBODY KNOWS WHAT GOD LOOKS LIKE. I HAVEN'T FINISHED DRAWIN' HIS PICTURE YET."

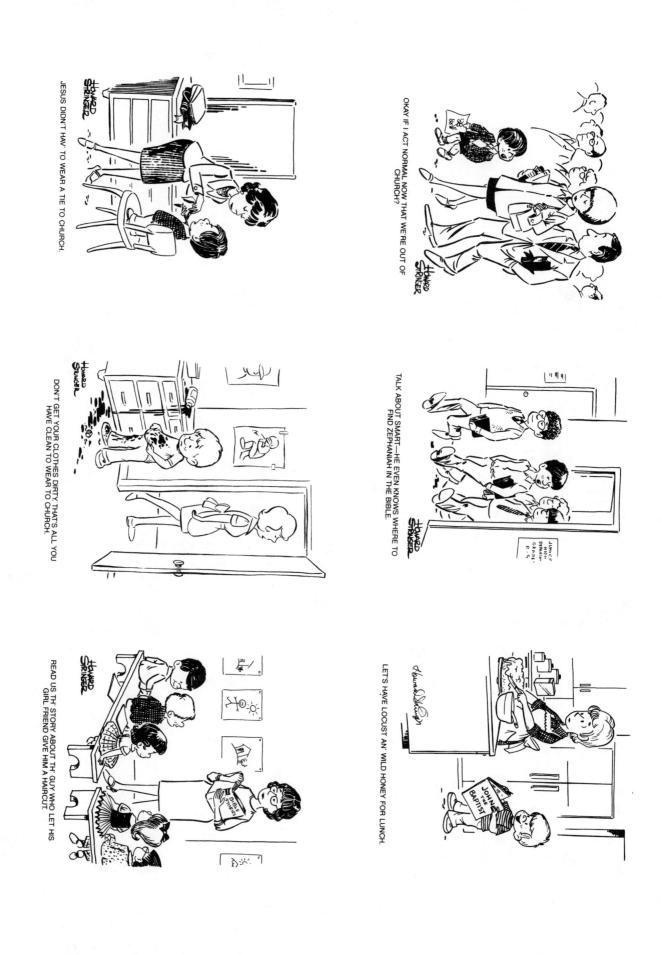

For the Very Young

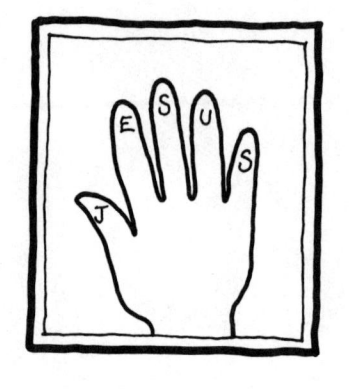

KEEP MY COMMANDMENTS

EXODUS 20:6

THE LORD SCATTERED THEM
OVER THE FACE OF THE
WHOLE EARTH

GENESIS 11:9

Thou shalt have no other gods before me. Exodus 20:3

WELL PLEASED

IN WHOM I AM

BELOVED SON

THIS IS MY

MATTHEW 3:17

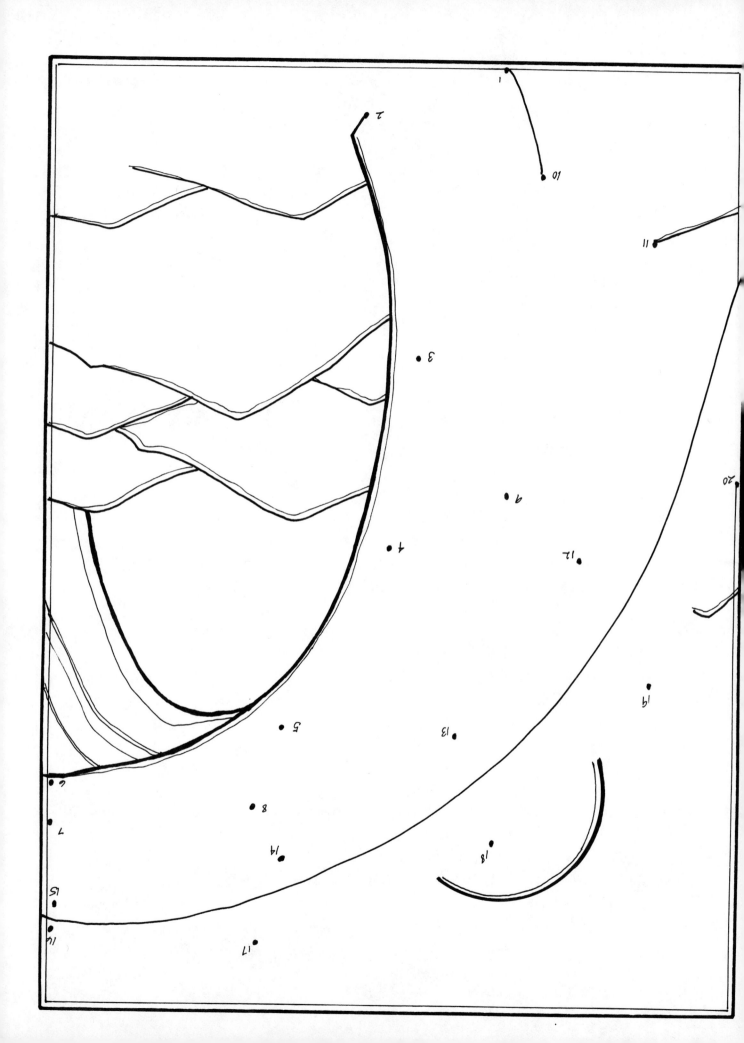

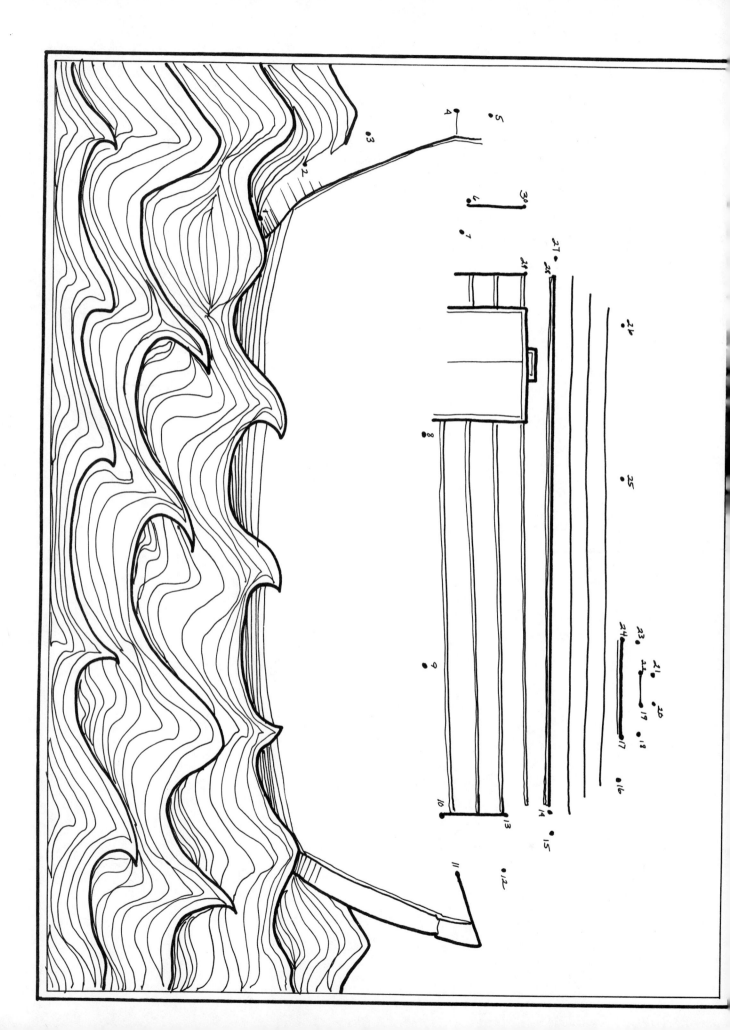

TEN COMMANDMENTS

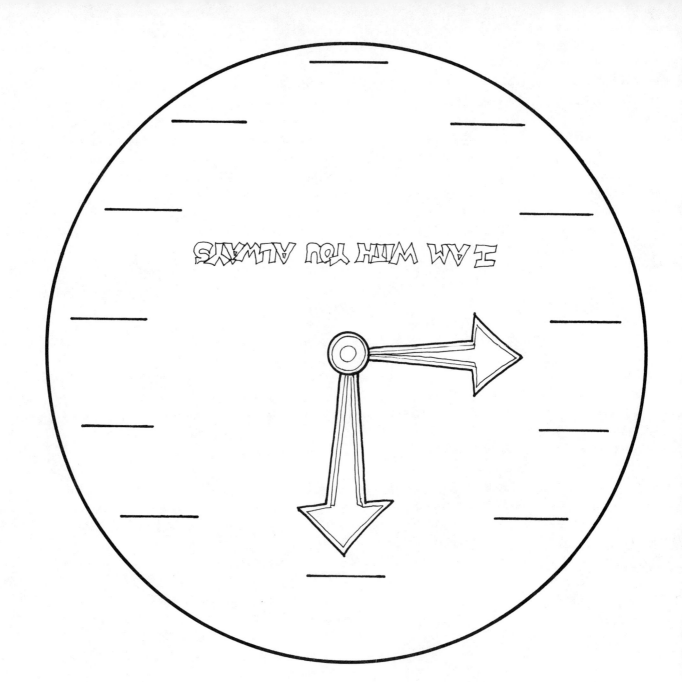

Write the numbers on the clock.

I AM WITH YOU ALWAYS

GOD IS WITH ME
ALL THE TIME

I am Jesus' helping hands

Trace your hand in the box. Next follow the
example and print a letter on each finger.
Whose name did you write?

Go tell it on the mountains

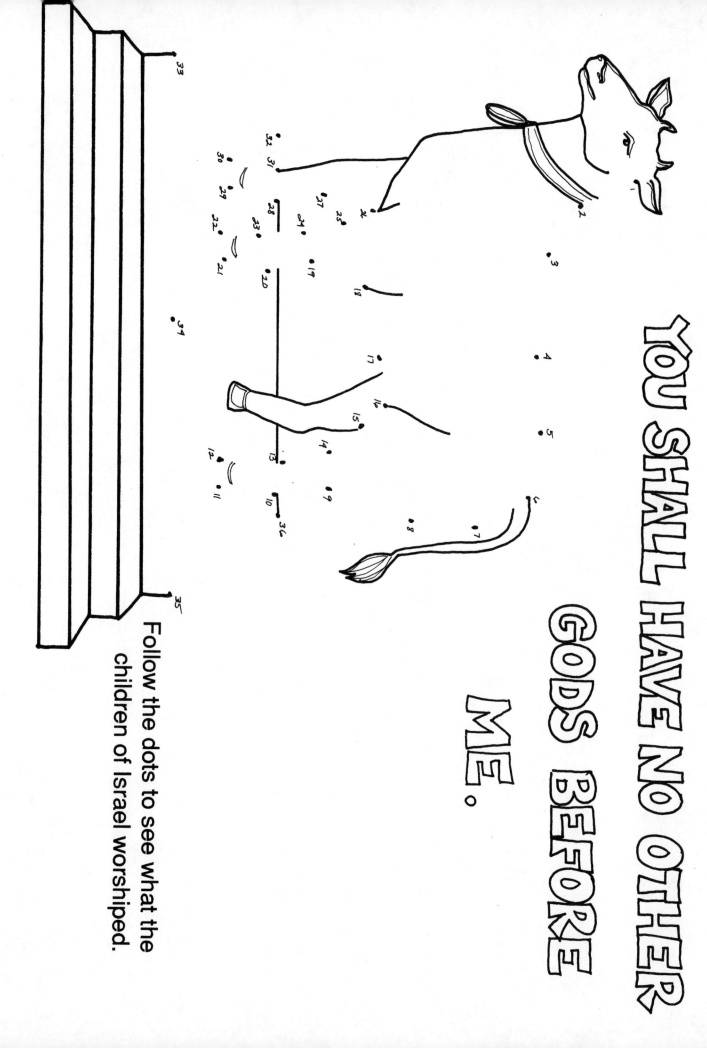

YOU SHALL HAVE NO OTHER GODS BEFORE ME.

Follow the dots to see what the children of Israel worshiped.

It's Mother's Day.
Make Mom a present by coloring in all the 1's.
Give her your present—and a big hug too!

Father's Day

I'm Daddy's child.
We are both God's
kids, God is is our
Father in Heaven.

Draw a picture of
you and your
daddy with Jesus.

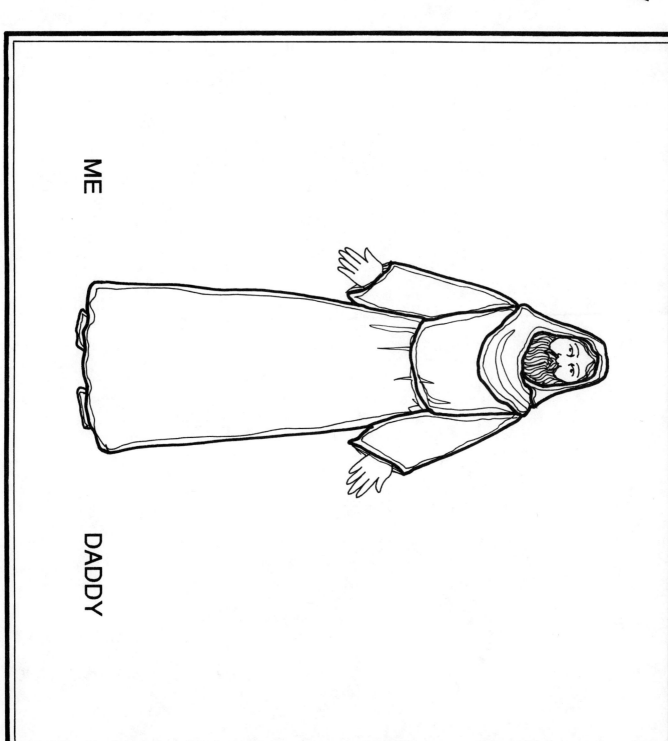

ME

DADDY

Draw faces on these pictures to show how you think Laurie felt.

Laurie wanted to go on a picnic.
It rained.
How did Laurie feel?

Then Laurie remembered God sends rain to help
the grass and flowers grow.
How did she feel now?

An angel talked to Mary and told her she was going to have
a baby. The angel told Mary to name the baby, Jesus.

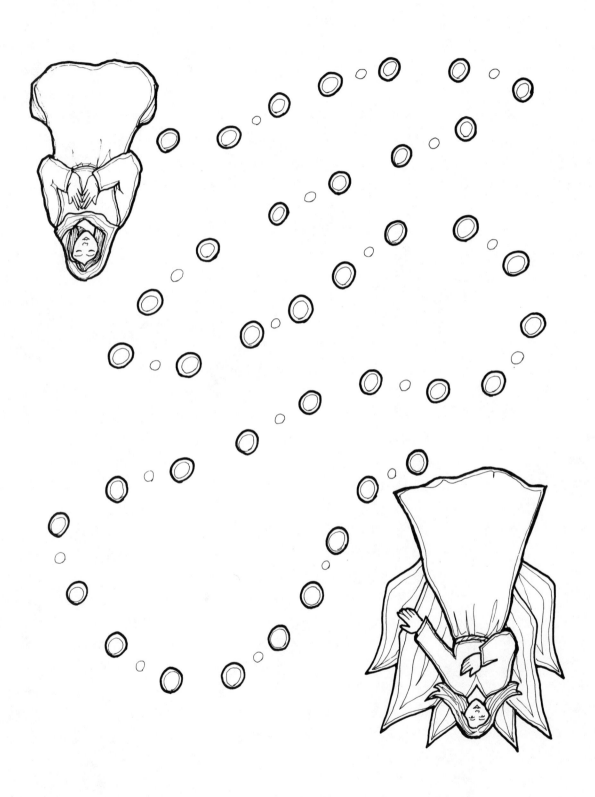

Follow the dots and help the angel get to Mary.

Dear Jesus, I bring my gift to You,
because I love You. Amen.

We bring our offerings to God as a way
of showing Him we love Him.

Draw some money in the offering plate.

When people die we feel sad, but we can feel happy too, becase they can live in heaven with Jesus.

Draw a face on John the way you think he feels.

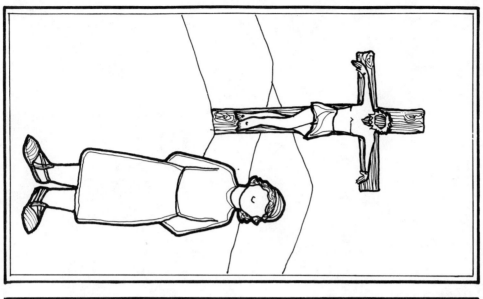
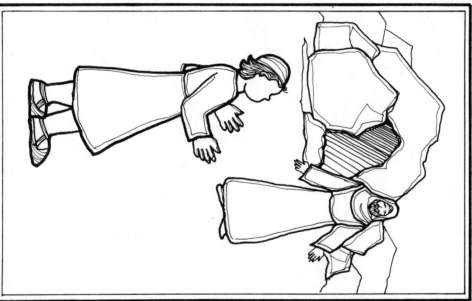
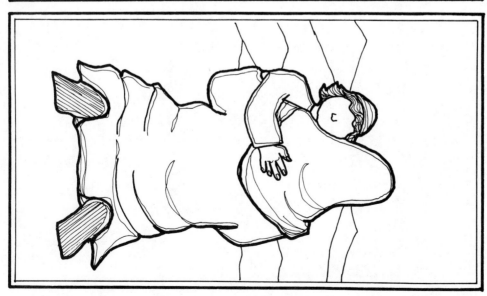

Just as the star led the wise men to the baby Jesus, so the Bible leads us to Jesus, our Lord and King.

Draw a star for the wise men.

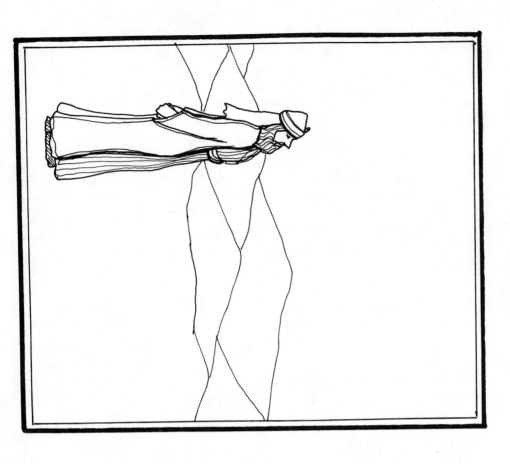

Draw a picture of you with this Bible.

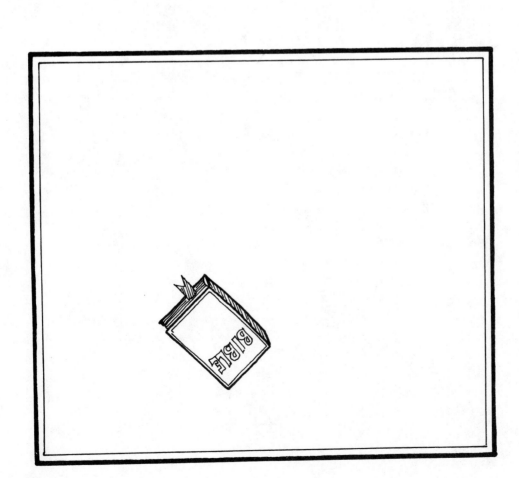

Jesus' First Miracle—
Changing Water into Wine

Circle the one that is different.

Things that make us think about Jesus

Draw a line to match the objects.

It's almost time for my first day of school. I'm excited, but I am scared too.
Then I remember Jesus is always with me!
I feel happy.

Draw a line through the path by matching like objects.

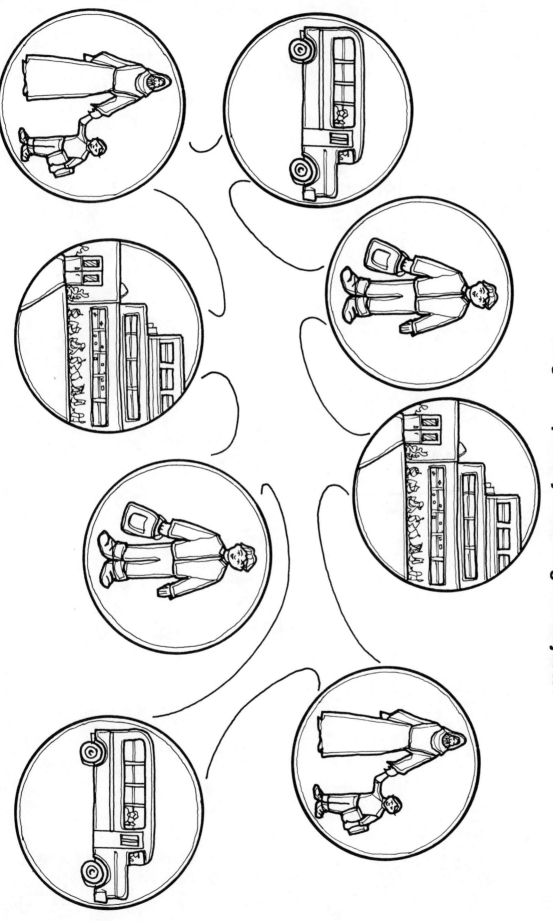

Valentine's Day

I smile because Jesus loves me!

Put your marker on the dotted line and follow it.

Start

Find the road the the Land of Canaan.

Jesus goes everywhere I go . . . even on vacation.
This makes me feel happy!

Draw some happy faces.

Dorcas was a lady in the Bible who made clothes for poor people.

Circle the coat that is different in each row.

Palm Sunday

Complete the dotted picture and you will see
the animal that Jesus rode on Palm Sunday.

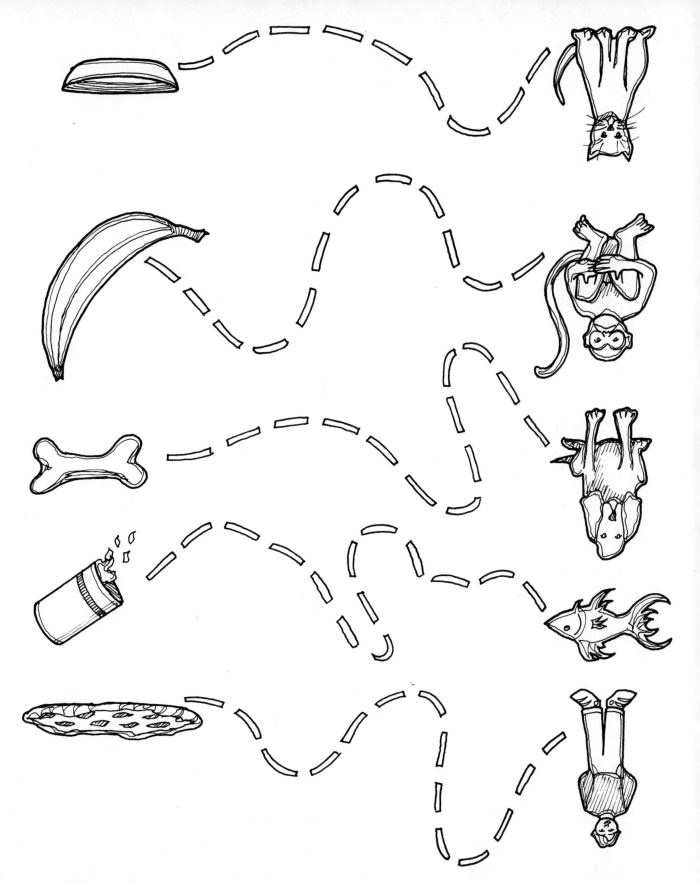

Place your marker on the object, then follow the line to the food.

Thank You, God, for the food we eat. Amen.

This do in remembrance of me.

The wise men followed a star to find the baby Jesus.

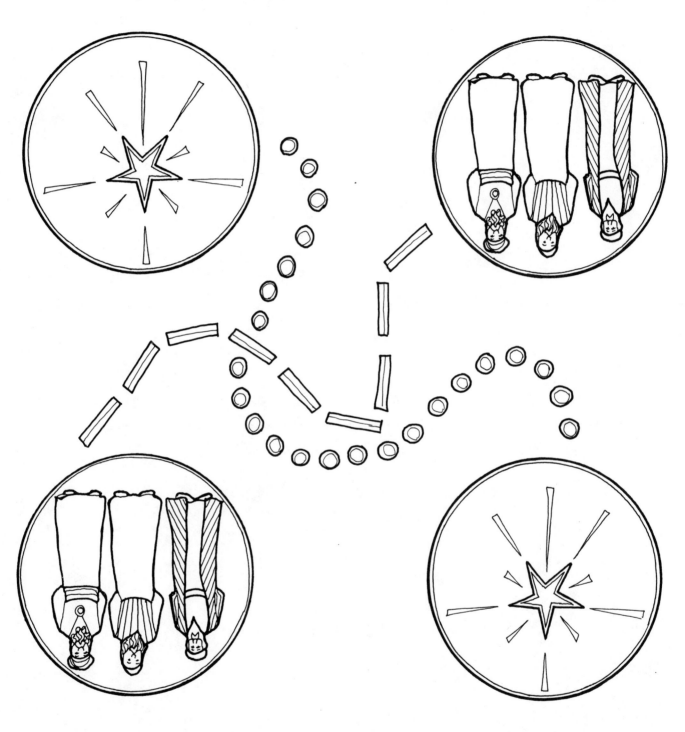

Follow the line to find a matching object.

Shepherds take care of sheep.
The shepherds went to see the baby Jesus.

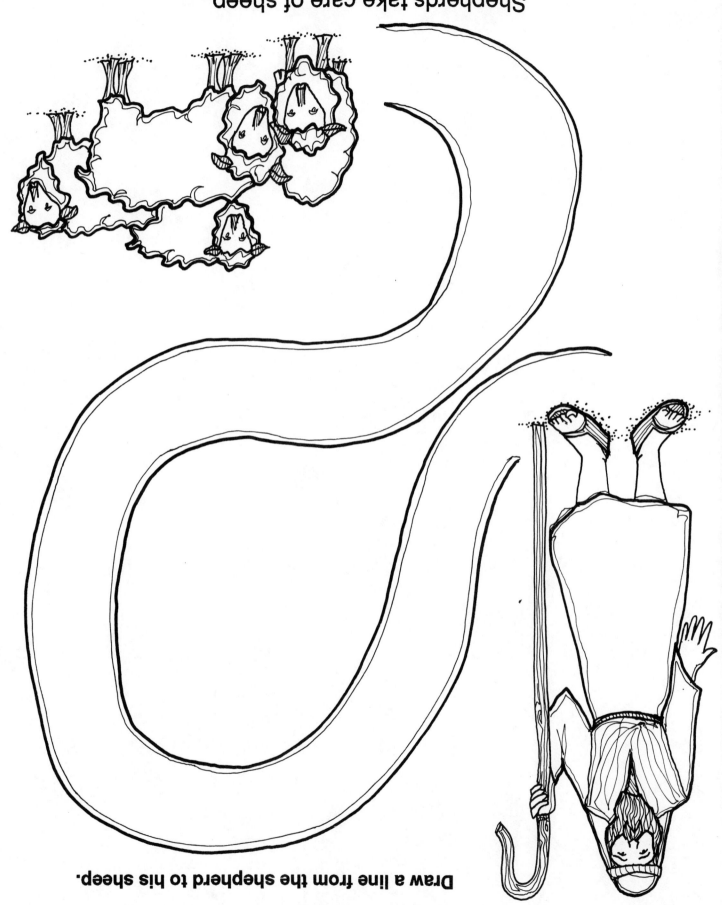

Draw a line from the shepherd to his sheep.

Draw a circle around each child who is hiding in the picture.

We can hide from each other, but we can't hide from God!

TRASH

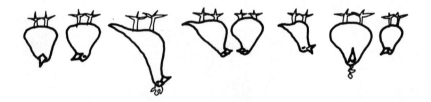

Art, Headings
Borders

CHILDREN'S BULLETIN
CHILDREN'S BULLETIN
CHILDREN'S BULLETIN
CHILDREN'S BULLETIN
CHILDREN'S BULLETIN
CHILDREN'S BULLETIN
CHILDREN'S BULLETIN
CHILDREN'S BULLETIN
CHILDREN'S BULLETIN
CHILDREN'S BULLETIN
CHILDREN'S BULLETIN
CHILDREN'S BULLETIN
CHILDREN'S BULLETIN
CHILDREN'S BULLETIN
CHILDREN'S BULLETIN
CHILDREN'S BULLETIN
CHILDREN'S BULLETIN
CHILDREN'S BULLETIN
CHILDREN'S BULLETIN
CHILDREN'S BULLETIN
CHILDREN'S BULLETIN
CHILDREN'S BULLETIN
CHILDREN'S BULLETIN
CHILDREN'S BULLETIN
CHILDREN'S BULLETIN
CHILDREN'S BULLETIN
CHILDREN'S BULLETIN
CHILDREN'S BULLETIN
CHILDREN'S BULLETIN
CHILDREN'S BULLETIN
CHILDREN'S BULLETIN
CHILDREN'S BULLETIN
CHILDREN'S BULLETIN
CHILDREN'S BULLETIN
CHILDREN'S BULLETIN
CHILDREN'S BULLETIN

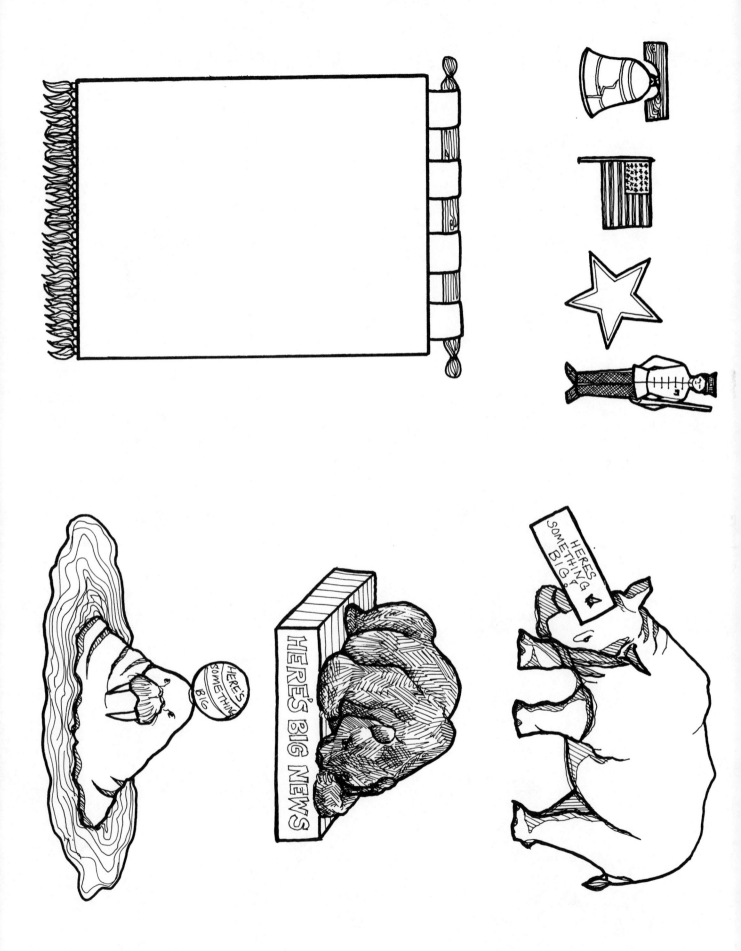

CHRISTMAS

THANKSGIVING DAY

GOOD FRIDAY

HAPPY BIRTHDAY AMERICA

ALL NATIONS

HERITAGE DAY

FOURTH
OF
JULY

ALL NATIONS
HERITAGE

ADVENT

FIRST WEEK:

ADVENT

SECOND WEEK:

ADVENT

THIRD WEEK:

ADVENT

FOURTH WEEK:

World
Hunger
Day

Hunger
Awareness
Week

Disability
Awareness
Sunday

World Hunger
Week

Bible
Sunday

We're glad you're
part of
God's Family
WELCOME!

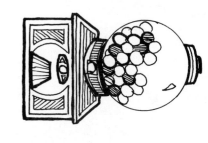

GOD CARES FOR HIS WORLD

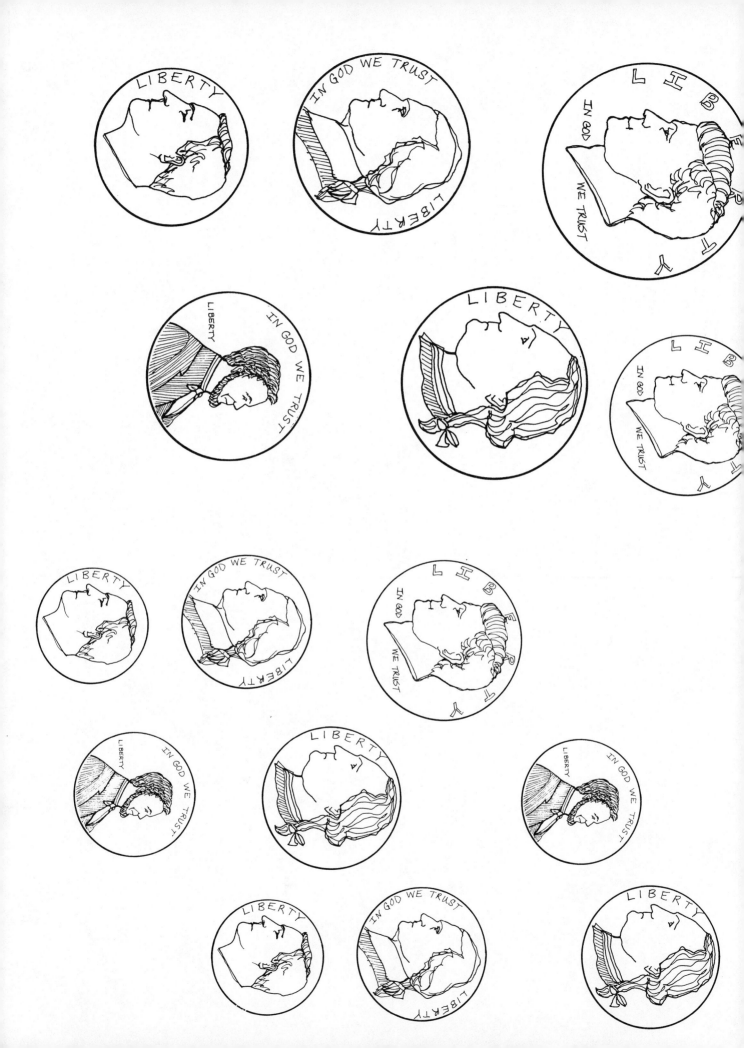

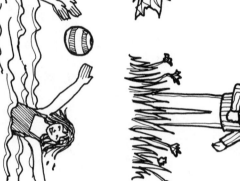

CHILDREN'S BULLETIN

CHILDREN'S BULLETIN

CHILDREN'S BULLETIN

CHILDREN'S BULLETIN

CHILDREN'S BULLETIN

CHILDREN'S BULLETIN

MISSION

EMPHASIS WEEK

Happy Birthday!

HAPPY MOTHER'S DAY

HAPPY FATHER'S DAY

BULLETIN BOARD

FAMILY TIME TABLE TALK

KNOW YOUR CHURCH FAMILY

MYSTERY PERSON

LABOR DAY

EASTER

MEMORIAL DAY

REFORMATION DAY

PENTECOST

ASCENSION DAY

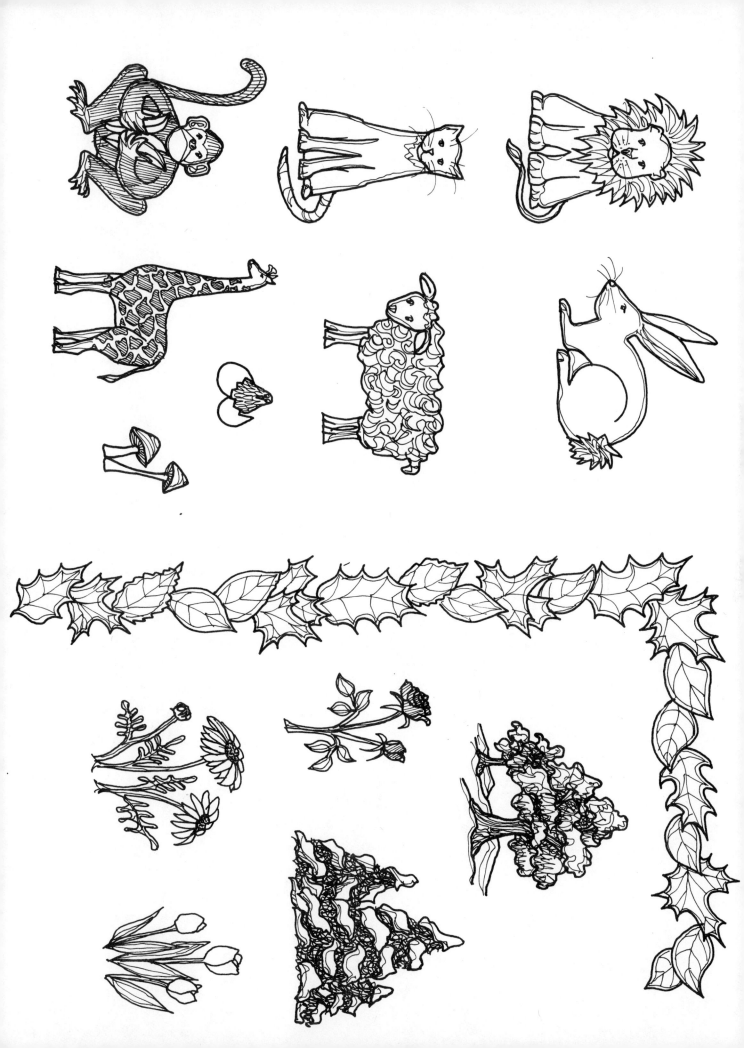

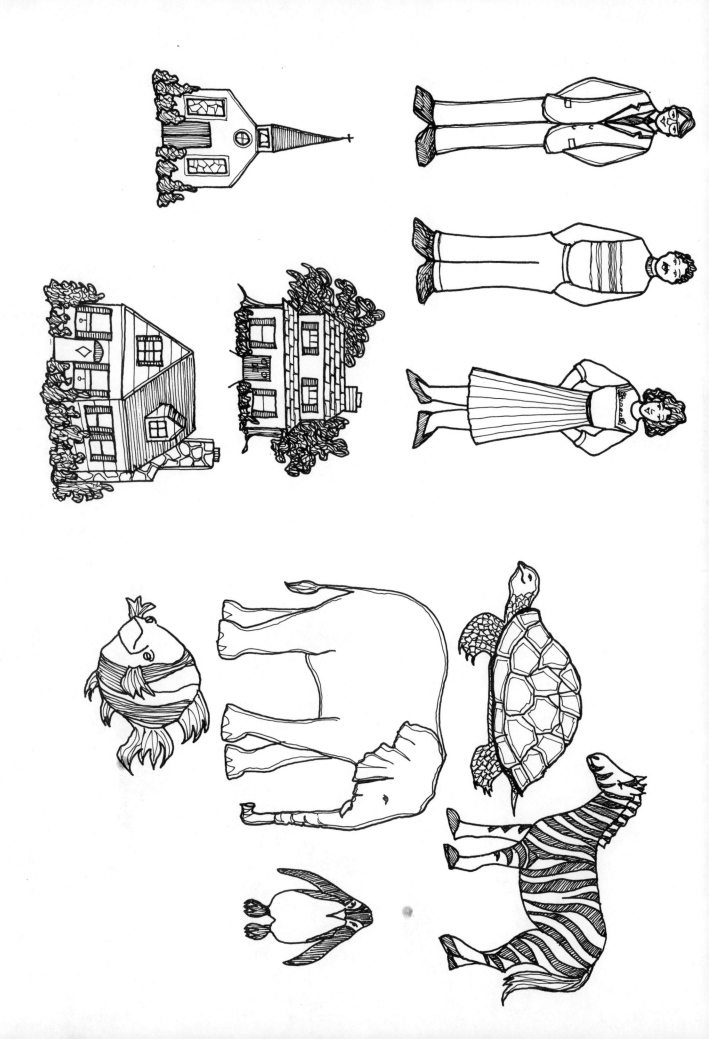

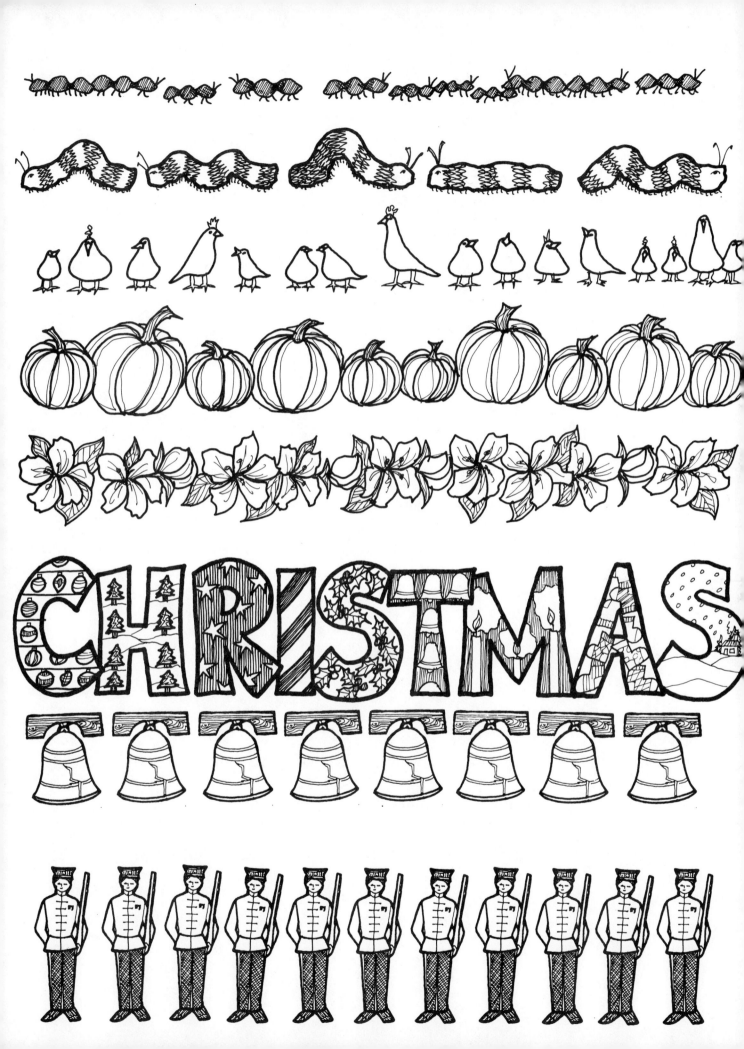

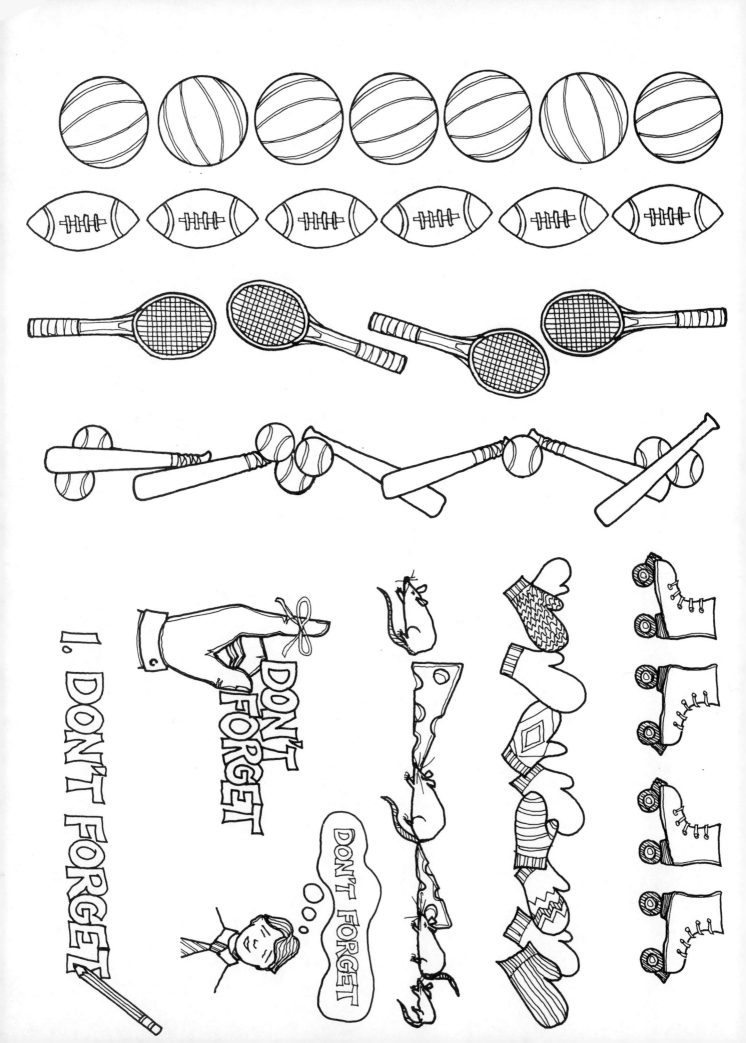